Copyright ©

ISBN 978-0-915545-16-2
First Printing 2013

Printed in the United States of America
All Rights Reserved!

Published by
Stanley R. Abbott Ministries, Inc.
P.O. Box 533
McRae, Georgia 31055
U.S.A.

Copyright

Preface

The need for called and gifted persons in the church today is really great! The fundamental building block of all ministry is to reveal Christ to the lost so they may know Him to be saved and to the church so they may know Him to grow to maturity. We need an increase in the revelation of Christ to all men!

There are so many devices of the enemy at work against the church on the earth today. People are tending to become more and more divided from one another. We must reverse this trend and begin to help the church enter new dimensions of unity. It is more than a little frightening to rehearse the words of Jesus regarding division.

> *"Every kingdom divided against itself is brought to desolation, and every city or house divided against itself will not stand."* **Matthew 12:25**

It is Jesus Himself who gave the offices of ministry! It is the Lord who gives each office revelation of Himself! It is Jesus as the Head of the church who sends these ministers out to impart the revelation He has given them to the sons of God. We absolutely must change our perspective of the offices, their purpose, and the results Jesus has designed them to produce. Perhaps if we can gain a better understanding of the purpose of the offices, the equipment of the offices, and known devices of the enemy hindering the function of the offices, we will be able to move forward more productively.

One thing is absolutely certain, Jesus is not going to change His plan for these offices of ministry. We are going to have to change our understanding of them in order to see the increase in the church for which we are looking. Because these offices of ministry are given by Christ as His will, He has a way for them to do His will!

Preface

Table of Contents

Chapter One
He Gave Some To Be — 1 - 16

Chapter Two
Called To Be — 17 - 32

Chapter Three
Equipment of the Ministries — 33 - 54

Chapter Four
Stewardship — 55 - 72

Chapter Five
Another Gospel — 73 - 86

Chapter Six
Teams, Teams, Teams — 87 - 96

Chapter Seven
Idealism, Tradition, & The Will of God — 97 -104

Summary & Conclusion — 105 - 112

Table of Contents

Chapter One

He Gave Some To Be

Our Father is a *"...giver..."!* This is part of His divine character, and it cannot be changed. He loves to give: He gave His only begotten Son to redeem mankind from sin and death. He gave His Spirit to comfort, teach, and guide us. He gives Eternal life to all who believe. He gives faith as a divinely empowered means of being born again and ability to fulfill our part of the new covenant. The array of things our God gives is vast. In fact, James writes...

> *"Every good gift and every perfect gift is from above, and comes down from the Father of lights, with whom there is no variation or shadow of turning."* **James 1:17**

John recorded the words Jesus spoke to Nicodemus revealing the motive for God's giving character.

> *"For God so **loved** the world that He gave..."* ***John 3:16***

God loves mankind! He always has, and He always will. This love for us motivates Him to desire good for us and to give those things necessary to help us obtain and achieve His will in our lives. Everything about our God's relationship with us is oriented to help us be a success in Him. He goes to extraordinary lengths to provide for us. The gift of His only begotten son is a perfect example of the lengths to which God will go to make provision for us because of His great love for us.

Making of a Ministry Gift

Although Jesus divested Himself of His divine attributes in order to become God's provision to redeem us, He still has His Father's character: ***Jesus is a giver!*** The purpose of this book is to consider the offices of ministry the Lord has *"...given..."* the church.

> *"And He Himself (Jesus) gave some to be apostles, some prophets, some evangelists, and some pastors and teachers, for the equipping (perfecting - KJV) of the saints, for the work of the ministry, for the edifying of the body of Christ; till we all come in the unity of the faith, and of the knowledge of the Son of God, to a perfect man, to the measure of the stature of the fullness of Christ; that we should no longer be children, tossed to and fro, and carried about with every wind of doctrine, by the trickery of men, in the cunning craftiness of deceitful plotting..."* ***Ephesians 4:12-14***

Jesus has given revelation of Himself to these ministries so they may give what they have freely received to us as God's sons so we may grow to maturity, to the measure of the stature of the fullness of Christ.

Because the enemy has also read this verse, he has seen the purpose of these ministries and has labored diligently to corrupt the truth about them in an effort to subvert their purpose. If these ministries fulfill their purpose accurately, the sons of God will reach maturity. That terrifies the enemy because he saw the life and works of Christ while He was on the earth, and he knows that all who believe are ordained to do the same works Jesus did. He wants to stop us from becoming like Christ as the way we live.

One of his main devices has been to sow subtle seeds of corruption into the church on the earth in an effort to alter the church's understanding of God's design and purpose for these ministries. The enemy's efforts have been frighteningly successful. A large majority of the church on the earth do not believe the offices of apostle and prophet are still viable for today. Much of the church who do believe in their contemporary viability have so significantly reduced the function of these offices that God's purposes for them have all but been thwarted.

For example, among many who believe in present day apostles, the office has been reduced to that of a church starter. By this defining purpose churches already started do not need the office. In many circles of those who believe the office of prophet still exists today, the office has become simply one who prophesies. Any believer who participates with the Holy Spirit to bring a *"...prophecy..."* to the church has falsely been labeled a prophet. Just because a believer receives inspiration to prophesy, that inspiration does not represent a calling to the office of prophet. This false defining purpose contradicts scripture which states *"...you can all prophesy..." (I Corinthians 14:31)*, but scripture also states, *"...Are all prophets?..." (I Corinthians 12:29)*. This rhetorical question *"...Are all prophets?..."* is actually making a statement that all are not prophets, although all can prophesy.

The efforts of the enemy have even caused the church to see the office of evangelist in a reduced role to just be responsible to win the lost to the Lord. Practically, that reduces his role to the church significantly since the church is comprised of those who have already received Jesus as Lord. In order to gain understanding of the ministries Christ has given to accurately reflect His purposes we must see them from His perspective. How did He intend for them to be provision to us?

A really important note must be made here. Deception is a terrible thing. Being deceived is awful. The subtle and crafty devices from the enemy have brought horrible corruptions of truth to the church. The statements regarding these corruptions are not accusations against the church but, rather, merely assessments of what can be currently seen as the practical reality of the offices of ministry within the church today. This assessment is not intended to be, nor is there any hidden agenda for it to become, a device of the enemy to accuse the brethren.

In his second letter to the church at Corinth Paul presented a significant understanding regarding at least one of the devices of the enemy using a specific illustration from among their members where forgiveness was needed.

> *"Now whom you forgive anything, I also forgive. For if indeed I have forgiven anything, I have forgiven that one for your sakes in the name of Christ, lest Satan should take advantage of us; for we are not ignorant of his devices..."* ***II Corinthians 2:10,11***

Paul is admonishing the church to extend forgiveness to a certain individual, which they know to be the will of God, so that

Satan would not have opportunity to take advantage of them. Then Paul makes a remarkable statement regarding the church's knowledge of Satan's devices. He wrote, *"...for we are not ignorant of Satan's devices..."*.

Even though Paul stated the church was not ignorant of Satan's devices, we read in a later portion of this same letter He was concerned about the minds of the church being corrupted from the simplicity that is in Christ.

> *"...I fear, lest somehow, as the serpent deceived Eve by his craftiness, so your minds may be corrupted from the simplicity that is in Christ..."* **II Corinthians 11:3**

Paul did not want Satan to take advantage of the church in any matter. He wrote, *"...I fear..." (for you)*. He did not want them to be deceived because he knew the subtle craftiness of the enemy.

Being ignorant of Satan's devices is one of the surest means for Satan to be able to take advantage of us. Just as Paul was certain the church at Corinth was ***not*** ignorant of Satan's devices, at least regarding the issue of forgiveness as we have already seen *(II Corinthians 2:10,11)*, I am certain much of the church today ***is*** ignorant of Satan's devices especially regarding the offices of ministry.

The motive for identifying corruptions of truth about the ministries Christ gave and showing how they have worked frighteningly successfully among us is to help awaken the church to the corruptions so we will not be taken advantage by them any longer. As long as the church continues to relate to the ministries Christ has given without being awakened to the corruptions about the offices, these corruptions as a device of the enemy will continue to work among us. Perhaps more importantly, the purposes of God for these ministries will not work accurately among us. The church will not grow to maturity to the measure of the stature of the fullness of Christ. **What a loss!**

Now, how did Jesus intend for these ministries to be provision to us? Our first step in answering this question is to determine the purpose why Jesus gave these ministries. Verse eleven of the fourth chapter of *Ephesians* identifies the ministries as apostles, prophets, evangelists, pastors and teachers. It is necessary to distinguish between the offices and the persons who have been called to stand in them.

For example, Paul identified himself in the opening greeting of several of the letters he wrote to the churches as an apostle. We see a number of different persons identified in the New Testament as apostles. The *"...persons..."* called to stand in the office of apostle were not the gifts Christ was giving to the church. The *"...office of apostle..."* was the gift to the church.

Christ has vested each office of ministry with certain equipment, revelation, and purpose. When a different person stands in the same office, the equipment, revelation, and purpose of the office does not change, just the person called to the office. Peter and Paul were both called to the office of apostle. Both had the same apostolic equipment, revelation, and purpose but were sent to different peoples. Their apostolic roles were the same even though they were each sent to different people groups. Without understanding the distinction between the offices as the gifts rather than the person standing in the office, the enemy will more easily be able to employ one of his devices against us. The church at Corinth demonstrates just such a corruption.

> *"And I, brethren, could not speak to you as to spiritual people but as to carnal, as to babes in Christ. I fed you with milk and not with solid food; for until now you were not able to receive it, and even now you are still not able; for you are still carnal. For where there are envy, strife, and divisions among you, are you not carnal and behaving like mere men? For when one says, 'I am of Paul,' and another says, 'I am of Apollos,' are you not carnal?"* **I Corinthians 3:1-4**

The Corinthians lost sight of the preeminence of Christ and the offices of ministry as the *"...gifts..."* Christ had given. Their carnal condition made them easy prey for the enemy to use one of his devices against them. ***It worked!*** The church began to be divided over which person of ministry with whom they desired to be identified. Paul uses two entire chapters, three and four of his first letter to the church, to address their folly and to give them opportunity to be restored back to a spiritual condition and to accurate revelation. In one verse he was actually inspired to instruct them, *"...let no one boast in men...".* If the enemy can use one of his devices to shift the focus of the church onto men, even men called to an office of ministry, and away from Christ, he will cause division in our midst.

Making of a Ministry Gift

> **We must no longer be ignorant of this device!**

> *"And He Himself gave some to be apostles, some prophets, some evangelists, and some pastors and teachers, for the equipping of the saints for the work of the ministry, for the edifying of the body of Christ, till we all come to the unity of the faith and of the knowledge of the Son of God, to a perfect man, to the measure of the stature of the fullness of Christ; that we should no longer be children, tossed to and fro and carried about with every wind of doctrine, by the trickery of men, in the cunning craftiness of deceitful plotting, but, speaking the truth in love, may grow up in all things into Him who is the head -- Christ-- from whom the whole body, joined and knit together by what every joint supplies, according to the effective working by which every part does its share, causes growth of the body for the edifying of itself in love."*
>
> **Ephesians 4:11-16**

There is an extremely high value on accurately understanding the purpose of the ministries and the interrelationship between them and those to whom they have been given. The function of these ministries is directly linked to the maturity of the saints, unity among the brethren, and growth of the body. Therefore, we absolutely must gain understanding of the purpose of these ministries. We must take great care as we receive revelation from our God regarding His design for these ministries that we do not incorporate any corruptions of the truth into our understanding. Christ Himself has given these gifts so we can expect them to be supernaturally equipped to fulfill their roles. Our job is to make sure we know what the purpose of those roles is so we may receive them correctly and maximize our benefit from their roles.

There are two distinctly different notions regarding the purpose of these ministries in relation to what is stated in verse twelve. After the offices are identified in verse eleven, verse twelve immediately states, *"...for the equipping of the saints for the work of ministry, for the edifying of the body of Christ..." (NKJV)*. The **King James Version** of the Bible punctuates these words differently, changing their meaning altogether. The **KJV** states, *"...for the perfecting of the saints, for the work of the ministry, for edifying of the body of Christ..."*.

The **NKJV** punctuation states the ministries have been given for *two* purposes:

    1. *"...for the equipping of the saints for the work of ministry,*
    2. *...for the edifying of the body of Christ..."*.

The **KJV** punctuation states the ministries have been given for *three* purposes:

    1. *"...for the perfecting of the saints,*
    2. *...for the work of the ministry,*
    3. *...and for edifying the body of Christ..."*.

I am fully persuaded the Lord Jesus does not want us to establish doctrine on the basis of the placement of a single grammatical punctuation mark, especially a comma. What you are about to read is an abbreviated presentation of revelation I believe I have received in these matters and the scriptural basis supporting that revelation. The revelation has three parts.

The first part of the revelation deals with God's purpose for redeeming us and our subsequent roles within His household. *Did our God redeem us to be His servants?* Consider the price our God paid for us. If He only wanted us to be His servants, would He have paid the price of His only begotten Son's life? Our God owns the cattle on a thousand hills. The earth and the fullness thereof is His. He could have more appropriately used some of the earth's resources, which are His anyway, in order to have purchased us. Scripture is replete with simple and clear statements about our redemption to be sons. Three of the simplest and most direct are *John 1:12,13*; *Romans 8:12-17*; and *Galatians 3:15-4:7*.

Abba did not redeem us to be His servants.
He redeemed us to be His sons!

We are to serve but from a position of love and sonship rather than as servants. Our priority must be loving our God as our Father rather than as our Master. The priority of His love for us is certainly as sons rather than servants.

The illustration of the eldest son in the *Parable of the Prodigal Son* taught us that doing the work for his father from a position of servant rather than son produced a disastrous result. Jesus as our illustration, on the other hand, taught us that having a priority of love and sonship motivated Him to faithfully do the work for His Father with a radically different result. He is the pattern we are to follow. His life as the model for our lives will produce an abundance of life, peace, and joy!

The second part of the revelation I received deals with the goal of the gifts as stated in **Ephesians 4:13**: *"...till we all come to the unity of the faith and of the knowledge of the Son of God, to a perfect man, to the measure of the stature of the fullness of Christ..."*. Scripture is telling us the goal is a unified church who has grown to maturity to the measure of the stature of the fullness of Christ. *What causes the sons of God to grow?* In Peter's first epistle he answers this question in his address to those who were newly born again.

> *"...as newborn babes, desire the pure milk of the word, that you may grow thereby..."* **I Peter 2:2**

Partaking of the word of God causes us to grow!
(...if partaken in faith as a spiritual people...)

Just prior to Jesus' arrest, trial, and crucifixion He prayed a most remarkable prayer in the presence of His disciples. In this prayer Jesus revealed the primary foundational component required for our growth.

> *"And this is eternal life, that they may know You, the only true God, and Jesus Christ whom You have sent."*
> **John 17:3**

Jesus is revealing this *"...eternal life..."* is available only in the knowledge of our God. Because our God is infinite we will be constantly growing in the knowledge of Him, and therefore, in *"...eternal life...".* In order for us to gain this knowledge Christ fills the ministries with it so they can impart it to us as the means for us to know Him and grow in eternal life.

Making of a Ministry Gift

Christ designed the offices of ministry to be provision to us by assigning each office the responsibility of a specific and unique revelation of Himself. Certain persons were *"...called..."* before the foundation of the world to stand in each of these offices. Christ reveals to those who have responded to their calling the specific and unique revelation which accompanies the office to which He has called them. He then sends these called and equipped ministers to reveal the knowledge of Christ from each of their respective offices to the sons of God as the means of *"...perfecting the saints..."*.

The offices of ministry have been given as gifts so we may know our God!

The third and final part of the revelation I received is oriented to the understanding the Holy Spirit presented through Paul's letters to the churches at Rome and Corinth.

> *"For I say, through the grace given to me, to everyone who is among you, not to think of himself more highly than he ought to think, but to think soberly, as God has dealt to each one a measure of faith. For as we have many members in one body, but all the members do not have the same function, so we, being many, are one body in Christ, and individually members of one another. Having then gifts differing according to the grace that is given to us, let us use them..."* **Romans 12:3-6**

> *"For as the body is one and has many members, but all the members of that one body, being many, are one body, so also is Christ. For by one Spirit we were all baptized into one body -- whether Jews or Greeks, whether slaves or free -- and have all been made to drink into one Spirit. For in*

> *fact the body is not one member but many. If the foot should say, 'Because I am not a hand, I am not of the body,' is it therefore not of the body? And if the ear should say, 'Because I am not an eye, I am not of the body,' is it therefore not of the body? If the whole body were an eye, where would be the hearing? If the whole were hearing, where would be the smelling? But now God has set the members, each one of them, in the body just as He pleased. And if they were all one member, where would the body be? But now indeed there are many members, yet one body. And the eye cannot say to the hand, 'I have no need of you.' No, much rather, those members of the body which seem to be weaker are necessary. And those members of the body which we think to be less honorable, on these we bestow greater honor; and our unpresentable parts have greater modesty, but our presentable parts have no need. But God composed the body, having given greater honor to that part which lacks it, that there should be no schism in the body, but that the members should have the same care for one another. And if one member suffers, all the members suffer with it; or if one member is honored, all the members rejoice with it. Now you are the body of Christ, and members individually. And God has appointed these in the church: first apostles, second prophets, third teachers...Are all apostles? Are all prophets? Are all teachers?..."*
>
> *I Corinthians 12:12-29*

The natural world illustration of a body and its parts is simple, clear, and easily understandable. The eyes, the ears, the nose, the feet, and the hands considered in this Scripture are all parts of the body, all having different functions within the body. Perhaps we could say they each have a unique *"...work..."* differing from one another. The eyes do not do the same *"...work..."* as the nose. The nose has its own *"...work..."* unique to the nose. The Holy Spirit inspired Paul to use these body illustrations, and then, immediately inspired him to begin considering the members of the body of Christ.

The natural body is parallel to Christ's flesh and bone body. That is, each member will have its own individual place unique from all the other parts. Then the Holy Spirit inspired Paul to consider God's appointment of ministries within the body of Christ, the church. He identifies some of them and then does a peculiar thing. He states that although God has appointed *"...some..."* to be apostles, *"...all..."* are not apostles. This same pattern is repeated for the other appointments in this list. If one person is called to be an apostle but others are not, then those who are called to be an apostle will have a certain *"...work of ministry..."* unique to the office. Others who are not called to this office will not have the same *"...work of ministry..."* as the one who has been called to the office. This same pattern will apply to all the ministries.

In the natural body, all are not noses or eyes because if they were, where would be the rest of the functions needed for the body? All of the individual parts of the natural body combined together, each doing its part, makes the whole body function as designed. So, too, when all of the parts of the body of Christ do their part according to what God has called them to be, the whole body will function as designed!

In the light of this illustration, the apostle has a *"...work of ministry..."* unique to his calling, the prophet has a *"...work of ministry..."* unique to his calling. This applies to all the ministries Christ has given. Therefore, one of the things listed in **Ephesians 4:12** as the purpose of the ministries, *"...for the work of the ministry..."*, is referring to the *"...work..."* each ministry has unique to that particular ministry. All do not have this same *"...work of the ministry..."* because all are not called to the ministry. Even those who are called do not have the same *"...work of ministry..."*.

He Gave Some To Be

Matthew recorded the words Jesus spoke to the multitudes and to His disciples during one particular time of ministry. On this occasion Jesus was addressing issues having to do with the *scribes* and *Pharisees*. At one point Jesus called the scribes and Pharisees...

> *"...Blind guides, who strain out a gnat and swallow a camel!..."* **Matthew 23:24**

In an effort to establish accurate understanding regarding anything from the Lord we must constantly guard against *"...straining out a gnat and swallowing a camel..."*. It is certainly not my intent to proceed by insisting you receive one interpretation of Scripture over another. However, like Paul *"...I fear..."* lest any members of the church be deceived by the subtle craftiness of the enemy. **Our desire is to know the truth!**

It is of the utmost importance to understand the purpose of the offices of ministry Christ has given us. Searching for or presenting understanding is certainly not *"...straining out a gnat and swallowing a camel..."*. If the ministries have been given to train us to do works of ministry, then we need to be trained thoroughly. If they are to reveal Christ to us so that we may know Him, then we need to receive completely! Ultimately, during every single encounter we have with any of the offices of ministry, we are going to decide how we will receive. We need to know Jesus' intent for the encounter rather than making such a decision randomly on our own.

For my eldest son's eighteenth birthday *(twenty years ago)* he asked me if I would go skydiving with him. I said I

Making of a Ministry Gift

would. *What was I thinking? Much younger then, and certainly more foolish!* In order for the skydiving company to allow us to make the jump, they required us to take a day of ground school training so we would be as prepared as possible before the actual jump. *As if one day of training will prepare you for skydiving.* During our ground school I repeatedly asked the *jump master* questions about some part of his training to make sure I understood. He never grew frustrated with my questions because he knew I was about to go up in a perfectly good airplane and jump out. He was more than delighted to help make sure I understood!

Everything is going to change when we view the connection of ministers with saints the same way we view student and jump master in a ground school pre-jump environment. Just *"...listening..."* to a person *"...teach..."*, even if it is something he has received from the Holy Spirit, is vastly different from receiving training from a person for a thing you actually intend to do: Especially, if the doing of that thing puts your life on the line. Being a doer of the word of God versus just listening to a *"...teaching..."* does indeed put your life on the line.

> *When the church has an accurate understanding of God's purpose for the gifts of ministry, everything is going to change!*

Chapter Two

Called To Be

Scripture clearly states that Jesus *"...Himself gave some to be apostles, some prophets, some evangelists, and some pastors and teachers..." **Ephesians 4:11**.* We know certainly, then, from where these offices of ministry have come. *Now, how does a person know whether he is one or not?*

It is essential that we have sound doctrine as the foundation for our Christian lives and for the successful operation of the church. Sound doctrine must be based on Scripture. The Holy Spirit inspired Paul to write:

> *"All Scripture is given by inspiration of God, and is profitable for **doctrine**, for reproof, for correction, for instruction in righteousness, that the man of God may be complete, thoroughly equipped for every good work."*
> **II Timothy 3:16,17**

It is too easy for our traditions and the doctrine of men to replace sound doctrine. Consider *"...tradition..."* in a Scriptural illustration of Jesus, His disciples, the Pharisees, and some of the scribes.

> *"Then the Pharisees and some of the scribes came together to Him, having come from Jerusalem. Now when they saw some of His disciples eat bread with defiled, that is, with unwashed hands, they found fault. For the Pharisees and all the Jews do not eat unless they wash their hands in a special way, holding the tradition of the*

> *elders. When they come from the marketplace, they do not eat unless they wash. And there are many other things which they have received and hold, like the washing of cups, pitchers, copper vessels, and couches. Then the Pharisees and scribes asked Him, 'Why do Your disciples not walk according to the tradition of the elders, but eat bread with unwashed hands?' He answered and said to them, 'Well did Isaiah prophesy of you hypocrites, as it is written: 'This people honors Me with their lips, but their heart is far from Me, and in vain they worship Me, teaching as doctrines the commandments of men.' For laying aside the commandment of God, you hold the tradition of men -- the washing of pitchers and cups, and many other such things you do. He said to them, "All too well you reject the commandment of God, that you may keep your tradition. For Moses said, 'Honor your father and your mother'; and, 'He who curses father or mother, let him be put to death.' But you say, 'If a man says to his father or mother, 'Whatever profit you might have received from me is Corban'--' (that is, a gift to God), then you no longer let him do anything for his father or his mother,* **making the word of God of no effect through your tradition which you have handed down***. And many such things you do."* **Mark 7:1-13**

The traditions and doctrine of men actually made the word of God of no effect! *Impossible?* Jesus Himself is the one giving us this understanding. Is tradition a bad thing then? Tradition is not a bad thing, but will most likely become a bad thing if it is not based on sound doctrine. Anything which causes the word of God to be of no effect must be stripped away from our lives and avoided altogether.

While serving the Lord as translation personnel and members of *Wycliffe Bible Translators* living in Papua New Guinea, my wife and I developed close friendships with other members from Australia. One particular story which emerged from our friendships regarding *tradition* was so profound it has remained in my memory for more than thirty five years.

Many of our Australian friends ate leg of lamb as their traditional Sunday lunch. While discussing the concept of traditions, one Australian friend recounted this story. A young Australian woman came of age and married. While at home one Sunday helping her mother prepare a leg of lamb, the young woman asked her mother, *"Why do you always cut off the end of the leg of lamb before cooking it?"* Her mother considered the question and replied, *"I don't know. I always saw my mother do it and just followed her example. Next time we are all together I will ask her."*

The next time they were all together the young woman's mother asked her mother the question. *"Why do you always cut off the end of the leg of lamb before you cook it?"* The woman immediately began to chuckle with a sparkle in her eye as she replied, *"When your father and I were first married, we didn't have much. The only pan we had was so small I had to cut off the end of the leg of lamb to fit it in the pan. I got so used to cutting the end off I continued even after we had a suitable sized pan."* They all laughed. Tradition can easily affect our daily lives in the natural world as well as in the church. Any tradition we have in the church must be based on sound doctrine in order to keep it from making the word of God of no effect.

Now, how does a person know whether he is one of these offices of ministry? And if he is, how does he know

Making of a Ministry Gift

whether he is an apostle, a prophet, an evangelist, a pastor, or a teacher?

Paul wrote thirteen epistles in the New Testament. In nine of those epistles he considered identifying his role to be of such significance he identified himself as an *"...apostle..."* in his opening greeting. A part of this identification process included the revelation it was by the will and commandment of God he had partaken of his role. In his letters to the church at Rome and Corinth he specifically stated he had been...

"...called (2822) to be an apostle of Jesus Christ ..."

2822 kletos from the same as *2821*; *invited*, i.e. *appointed*, or (spec.) a *saint*: -- called.

Strong's Exhaustive Concordance of the Bible

The most significant understanding we gain from Paul's life and ministry is that he was an apostle by the will and commandment of God which had been conveyed through a specific *"...calling..."* from God. Since Jesus has been given all authority in heaven and on earth *(Matthew 28:18)*, has been appointed to be head over all things to the church, which is His body *(Ephesians 1:22,23)*, and has given the offices of ministry as gifts *(Ephesians 4:11)*, it is not a stretch to establish as truth that Jesus is the One who called Paul to the role of apostle.

A person can only hold an office of ministry by the will and commandment of God conveyed through a specific calling from the Lord Jesus. Being an apostle, prophet, evangelist, pastor, or teacher is by invitation only! It is the calling of God which opens the door to the authority and anointing of any of these offices.

Without knowing the office to which you have been called it is virtually impossible to provide successful supernatural ministry to the church as God intended. It would be very similar to being a part of a business in the natural world without knowing your specific role. Successful businesses are successful in large part because everyone within the business knows their role and fulfills it to the best of their ability. It is not enough simply to be a part of a business without knowing your role. You must know precisely what your part is in order to do your part.

In today's political climate it may be counterproductive to use a political illustration. However, I am confident the *"...point..."* of the illustration can be made without being lost in today's politics. Can you imagine politicians elected in generic terms? That is, as many politicians as are required to run a city, county, state, or nation all elected in mass numbers without any office specified other than politician. How would these elected politicians know what to do in their newly elected position of politician? How could anyone determine who would fulfill the mayor, or governor, or president's responsibilities if the politicians were not specifically elected to one of those offices?

Similarly, how would ministers fulfill the roles of apostle, prophet, evangelist, pastor, or teacher if they did not

Making of a Ministry Gift

know the office to which they had been called. Tradition too often has insisted, *"It is enough just to believe the Lord has called you to the ministry. You do not need to know the specific office, just get busy doing the work of the ministry."* How is that possible since the work of the ministry is specifically oriented to a specific office of ministry? Perhaps it is enough to know you are called to the ministry in general terms to help you transition from the secular world to the world of ministry. This time of transition would include some type of ministerial training. However, at some point the one called is going to have to learn the specific office to which he has been called in order to be able to do his work of the ministry.

I have enjoyed a quote from Mother Theresa for many years. She is quoted as having said:

> *"You can do what I cannot do.*
> *I can do what you cannot do.*
> *Together we can do great things."*

Living this philosophy as a way of life was seen by the world as so powerfully productive she was awarded the 1979 Nobel Peace Prize. Perhaps she knew something about the need to properly identify roles.

Although called by God, I did not know that I was called, acknowledge that calling, or accept it until I was thirty years old. When I did acknowledge the calling, I did not have any idea what to do next so I called a minister I knew to share my news and to ask for help. This minister said the first thing

Called To Be

I needed to do was get prepared and the best way to do that was to go to Bible School. He said a good friend of his was in the process of starting a Training Center which he would recommend highly. I received all the necessary information, made contacts, completed application, and moved across the country to attend the charter class of this new Training Center.

Upon successfully completing one year of training, I *(we, my wife and I)* was no closer to knowing to what I had been called than before I started the year of training. Oh, I had learned about calling, offices of ministry, and general purposes, but I did not have a *"...clue..."* to which office I had been called or my purpose of ministry! A door clearly opened for us to become members of **Wycliffe Bible Translators**. Another two years of training including linguistic, translation, and jungle training. Then off to Papua New Guinea to select a language group for us to begin applying our linguistic, translation, and jungle living skills.

After two years of living with people only one generation removed from cannibalism in a mangrove swamp in a grass house doing linguistic and translation work all day every day, I began to question my ministerial role. I *"...knew..."* I *(my wife, too)* was called to the ministry, but I could not find Bible translator anywhere in the Bible. I could stretch my imagination to see us as missionaries, but I knew deep inside of my heart that my personal and current ministerial role was not to be my ultimate role.

Making of a Ministry Gift

My next step launched a process which would change everything. I began to search with all my being for my ultimate ministry. The process was excruciatingly painful. It is as if I was lost in the jungles of Papua New Guinea, and my search was fruitless. Finally, the Lord Jesus began to speak to me. He said, *"Your search is bringing harm to you and causing you to be ineffective at doing what I sent you here to do."* He then asked me two questions and set me on a course that was to be the course I would follow again and again for the remainder of my ministry life. He asked, *"Do you believe you are where I have sent you? ...and doing what I have asked you to do?"* I answered yes to both questions. Both my wife and I believed the **Wycliffe** door was the door the Lord had opened. The next words out of His mouth set my course! He said, *"I am putting you on a one-day-at-a-time program. I want you to rise in the morning and do what your hand finds to do. If I choose to change your direction, I will do so in the morning"*.

For the next two years I lived on this one-day-at-a-time program. I cannot say it took away my angst regarding my ultimate ministerial role, but at least it removed my lack of productivity regarding my **Wycliffe** role and restored the peace I had lost regarding **Wycliffe** as the door of the Lord. My one year of training at the Bible Training Center, our two years of **Wycliffe** training, and now our four years of field training in Papua New Guinea provided seven years of experience and served as transition to take us out of the secular world and into the world of ministry.

Called To Be

Just before we were set to go home on furlough we received a letter from a ministry in the U.S.A. As I opened the letter, even before I had a chance to read it, the Lord said, *"Attach yourself to this chariot"*. The letter was asking if I would consider moving back to the U.S.A. and help start a missions program for this ministry and be the Missions Director. It did not really matter what the request had been. The Lord had already spoken and was changing my direction that very morning.

My wife and I were in agreement that this was the door of the Lord. We immediately started the process of resigning from **Wycliffe**, packing up our village home, and returning back to the U.S.A. to live. The next few months were a blur. We went from living in a grass house in a mangrove swamp in Papua New Guinea to owning our own home in the suburbs in the U.S.A. We did not bring a single fork, knife, or spoon back from Papua New Guinea, the Lord supplied all new *"...stuff..."* for our relocation. We ain't in Kansas no more, Dorothy! Our lives were just like Dorothy's, caught up in a giant whirlwind.

Shortly after assuming my new role while driving down the street one day, the Lord asked me a very peculiar question. I was confident it was the Lord's voice because part of my *one-day-at-a-time program* back in Papua New Guinea had included instructions to develop my spiritual communication skills. I was instructed to pray in tongues every day a specified amount of time with nothing else as my focus during that prayer time. For the first two years and ever since I have worked diligently at developing these skills.

Making of a Ministry Gift

The Lord asked, *"Do you think a bird knows he is a bird?"*

Somewhat puzzled, I nevertheless quickly answered because I knew it was the Lord asking, *"No Lord, I do not believe a bird knows he is a bird. He just is what he is"*.

The Lord continued, *"Well, when the bird is first hatched, he lies in the nest without feathers, does not know how to fly, dig for worms, or make a nest. He does not know how to do any of the things a bird does except eat and sleep, and, yet, he is still a bird. Then one day after the mother bird teaches him all the things he must know as a bird, he graduates from the nest to go off on his own. Do you think on his graduation day he comes into some kind of awareness that he is a bird?"*

I said, *"No, Lord, he is just what he is"*.

The Lord was helping me to understand that a person, like the bird not knowing he is a bird, can be called to the ministry but not know that he is called or for what purpose he is called. Then the Lord taught me about ministers from the Bible having been called before the foundation of the world: Isaiah, Jeremiah, and the Lord Himself *(Isaiah 49:1-5; Jeremiah 1:4,5; I Peter 1:18-20)*. He even showed me how all believers had been called with a holy calling even before time began *(II Timothy 1:9)*.

This was not a Bible study where I was researching the topic of *"...calling..."*. I was driving down the street and the Lord was teaching me. When He is doing the *"...teaching..."* there is a supernatural anointing available for the one being taught to *"...understand..."*. Although I was benefiting from this anointing, He still allowed me to ask questions.

Then the Lord showed how Paul had accepted his calling in the process of the Damascus Road experience including the street called Straight involvement with Ananais *(Acts 9:1-22)*. He taught me how Paul had not known that he was called to preach Christ among the Gentiles from the very moment he was separated from his mother's womb *(Galatians 1:15,16)*. He taught me how Paul had operated in full-time ministry for a number of years as a prophet and / or teacher *(Acts 13:1)*, not as an apostle.

Acts 13:1 says, *"...in the church that was at Antioch there were certain prophets and teachers: Barnabas, Simeon, Lucius, Manaen, and Saul..."*. This same phrasing could be used referring to *"...men and women..."*. For example, *"...in the church that was at Antioch there were certain men and women..."*. The phrase *"...certain men and women..."* in this example would be saying that both men and women were present, certainly not that everyone present was both a man and a woman.

It is not clear whether Barnabas, Simeon, Lucius, Manaen, and Saul were all prophets and teachers or whether some were prophets and others teachers. The only thing which is clear is that the five persons present all fell into the category of prophets and teachers, just like you and I would all fall into the category of men and women. Then, He showed me according to God's timing, the Holy Spirit opened the door for Saul of Tarsus to identify his apostolic calling and enter

Making of a Ministry Gift

his apostolic role. From that time forward Saul of Tarsus became known as Paul *(Acts 13:1-and following)*.

I was exhilarated by the presence of the Lord and by the exchange between us. Our topics up to this point had been about other people and their offices of ministry. Then suddenly it changed; the Lord made it personal. He said, *"I have called you to the office of apostle."* Having lived on the one-day-at-a-time program for well over two years, I can say honestly that I was not prepared for this pronouncement. I had already determined the office to which I desired to be called: *Teacher*. I had my ministry all planned. I would rent meeting rooms in hotels and motels teaching the hungry sons of God. Oh, what a plan. The office of apostle did not fit into my plans.

I had been taught *"...about..."* the office of apostle and actually knew of a couple of ministers who were identified as apostles. These ministers had been in ministry for 1,000 years, started a million churches, and written enough books to fill the Library of Congress. Besides all that, I had been taught that you could not identify yourself as an apostle or prophet. You could call yourself a pastor, teacher, or evangelist. That was okay, but not apostle or prophet. If others identify you as such that is acceptable, but most certainly you cannot identify yourself as such.

I did not want anything to do with this office. For several weeks I wrestled with the Lord in an effort to *"...get out of..."* the calling to *"...this office..."*. Finally, the Lord said,

Called To Be

"This is not a negotiation. This office is My choice for you. You can either accept it or reject it, but there is no other choice". I accepted it but did not like it. It took me another ten years or so before I saw how impossible it was to stand in an office successfully without fully embracing it.

It seems strange that if a person enters the ministry on the basis of having been called by God, and God's calling is what makes a person a pastor, teacher, or evangelist, then isn't it God's calling that makes a person an apostle or a prophet? And if it is God's calling that makes a person an apostle, prophet, evangelist, pastor, or teacher and not what a person does, then surely a person is no more an apostle, prophet, evangelist, pastor, or teacher at the end of his ministry than at the beginning! Scripture inspired by God the Holy Spirit seems to support this premise.

> *"Then the word of the Lord came to me, saying: 'Before I formed you in the womb I knew you; before you were born I sanctified you; I ordained you a prophet to the nations.' Then said I: 'Ah, Lord God! Behold, I cannot speak, for I am a youth.' But the Lord said to me: 'Do not say, 'I am a youth,' For you shall go to all to whom I send you, and whatever I command you, you shall speak. Do not be afraid of their faces, for I am with you to deliver you,' says the Lord. Then the Lord put forth His hand and touched my mouth, and the Lord said to me; 'Behold, I have put My words in your mouth. See, I have this day set you over the nations and over the kingdoms, to root out and to pull down, to destroy and to throw down, to build and to plant.'* **Jeremiah 1:4-10**

Before Jeremiah was born God had already *"...sanctified and ordained him to be a prophet..."*. Even as a youth

Making of a Ministry Gift

God placed him *"...over nations and over kingdoms..."*. It is clearly the calling of God which causes a person to be a minister and as a minister to be able to fulfill the office of God's choosing.

The enemy uses one of his most subtle but deadly devices against the church in such matters in an effort to stop the will of God from working in our lives. He collects and reports abuses of the gifts perpetuated by unscrupulous and uncalled people or, at the very least, immature and foolish believers. Then he creates a *"...fear syndrome..."* among us causing us to see the dark folly of these abuses and tries to make us believe it is our responsibility to prevent future abuses.

I have heard that treasury agents are trained by teaching them to identify real dollar bills so that when they see a counterfeit bill, they can more easily see that it is not the real bill. Whether true or not I cannot say, but the principle is very valid. If we taught believers to know the will of God and demonstrated that will, then when believers saw the work of the enemy, it would be easier for them to distinguish it from God's will.

Let's teach accurately, accept our true callings from the Lord, and learn to walk in them successfully. Then when an unscrupulous, or uncalled, or immature, or foolish person impersonates the true gifted and called minister, the church will see the difference, accepting the true and rejecting the false. No matter which of the offices to which a person is called, it is only the calling of God which grants entrance into the office and the anointing from God which empowers the person to fulfill the responsibilities of the office to which he has been called!

Be who He has called you to be!

Making of a Ministry Gift

Chapter Three

Equipment of the Ministries

We have already established it is of the utmost importance to understand the purpose of the offices of ministry, whatever that may be. Different versions of the Bible have used different grammatical punctuations for *Ephesians 4:12* regarding the purposes for the ministries identified in *Ephesians 4:11*. This difference in punctuation causes the purposes for these ministries to *appear* to be different.

> *"And He Himself gave some to be apostles, some prophets, some evangelists, and some pastors and teachers..."*

1. *"...for the equipping of the saints for the work of ministry, for the edifying of the body of Christ..." (**NKJV**)*

2. *"...for the perfecting of the saints, for the work of the ministry, for the edifying of the body of Christ. (**KJV**)*

Although we can see how two distinctly different notions regarding the purpose of the ministry gifts could be established on the basis of the placement of a comma, hopefully, we are agreed the Lord Jesus does not want us to establish doctrine on the basis of a single grammatical punctuation mark.

With just a small step together we can achieve a level of agreement which will cause a great surge in the spirit. Doing *"...the work of ministry..."* is an act of service no matter who does it. We have already stated, *"We are to serve but from a position of love and sonship rather than as servants. Our priority must be loving our God as our Father rather than as our Master. The priority of His love for us is certainly as sons rather than servants."* If we begin with the revelation that our redemption made us sons of God rather than servants of God *(See **John 1:12,13**; **Romans 8:12-17**; and **Galatians 3:15-4:7**),* we can build on this foundational understanding. Building on this foundation can begin easily with the revelation contained in the words of the Lord recorded by John:

> *"No one has ascended to heaven but He who came down from heaven, that is, the Son of Man who is in heaven. And as Moses lifted up the serpent in the wilderness, even so must the Son of Man be lifted up, that whoever believes in Him should not perish but have eternal life. For God so loved the world that He gave His only begotten Son, that whoever believes in Him should not perish but have everlasting life."* **John 3:13-16**

> *"Father, the hour has come. Glorify Your Son, that Your Son also may glorify You, as You have given Him authority over all flesh, that He should give eternal life to as many as You have given Him. And this is eternal life, that they may know You, the only true God, and Jesus Christ whom You have sent."* **John 17:1-3**

While many Scriptures could be quoted about the purpose for Jesus coming to the earth, perhaps all of them could be encapsulated in one simple understanding...

> ***God's desire for man to know Him so that man could live and not die!***

Equipment of the Ministries

God's desire for man to know Him as the means of living and not dying begins with new birth but is not limited to being born again. Believers' growth in the knowledge of God causes new measures of the life of God to replace the old measures of death that has ruled in our lives.

We actually grow in the life of God!

Every aspect of Jesus' ministry was to reveal the Father! According to the words of Jesus in His prayer to His Father *(John 17:3)*, the revelation of God is what gives man opportunity to know God, and knowing God is what causes man to partake of eternal life which is life like God has it. **This, then, becomes the fundamental building block of all ministry** no matter who does the work thereof. Whether you are an apostle, prophet, evangelist, pastor, teacher, or non-ministry-gift-believer **"...all work of ministry is to reveal Christ..."** so others may know Him in order to partake of the very life of God whether as the initial entrance into the kingdom or growth as a believer.

With a simple agreement on these foundational truths we can move forward free of division in the manner about which Paul wrote to the church at Corinth...

> *"Now I plead with you, brethren, by the name of the Lord Jesus Christ, that you all speak the same thing, and that there be no divisions among you, but that you be perfectly joined together in the same mind and in the same judgment."* ***I Corinthians 1:10***

Making of a Ministry Gift

Every aspect of the church on the earth will revolve around revealing Christ.

Believers knowing Christ and making Him known will be "...for the edifying of the body of Christ..."!

While it is easy to see how every member of the body of Christ has a part in revealing Christ, the seed from which this revelation begins is the offices of ministry. Christ Jesus gave the offices of ministry *"...for the perfecting (2677) of the saints...".* This perfecting process is to bring the saints *"...the knowledge of the Son of God, to a perfect (5046) man, to the measure of the stature of the fullness of Christ...".*

> **2677 katartismos** from *2675*; *complete furnishing* (obj.): -- perfecting.
>
> **5046 teleelos** from *5056*; *complete* (in various applications of labor, growth, mental and moral character, etc.); neut. (as noun, with *3588*) *completeness*: -- of full age, man, perfect.
>
> ***Strong's Exhaustive Concordance of the Bible***

Revelation of Christ is the primary component of the ministries so they may be able to fulfill their roles. Each office has been given a unique and specific revelation of Christ. When the offices of ministry have collectively given this knowledge to the saints, if the saints have received it in faith and have been doers of the word as spiritual people, they will be *"...perfect...",* that is of full age, mature spiritual men.

Equipment of the Ministries

It is important to note here a person called to one of these ministries does not begin to minister revelation of Christ to the saints in an effort to determine to which office he has been called. Instead, Jesus, the One who calls the person to stand in an office of ministry is responsible to identify the office to which the person has been *"...called..."*. It is absolutely accurate to say the revelation a minister gives to others corresponds to whatever office of that particular minister but office first, then consistent giving of revelation. This identification process is crucial for the person called to know his role of ministry, to receive the revelation of Christ necessary to fulfill this role, and so the saints may be able to know how to relate to him.

Jesus has designed the church to operate by certain spiritual principles. One of those principles deals with how we are to relate to one another. Accurate acceptance of one another opens the door to the supernatural. Receiving one another as mere men closes the door on the supernatural.

> *"He who receives you receives Me, and he who receives Me receives Him who sent Me. He who receives a prophet in the name of a prophet shall receive a prophet's reward. And he who receives a righteous man in the name of a righteous man shall receive a righteous man's reward. And whoever gives one of these little ones only a cup of cold water in the name of a disciple, assuredly, I say to you, he shall by no means lose his reward."*
> **Matthew 10:40-42**

A situation which occurred during Jesus' earthly ministry provides us with the most wonderful illustration of this principle.

Making of a Ministry Gift

> *"He (Jesus) came to His own, and His own did not receive Him. But as many as received Him, to them He gave the right to become children of God, to those who believe in His name..."* **John 1:11,12**

Many of the people to whom Jesus was sent refused to see Him as anything more than just a mere man. Their refusal to receive Him as *"...from God..."* closed the door on their provisions from heaven. God was not withholding their provisions they were stopping their provisions. When the people received Jesus as *"...from God..."*, heaven's provisions were released. Their actions opened the windows of heaven on their own behalf.

Nicodemus came to Jesus by night saying...

> *"...Rabbi, we know that You are a teacher come from God; for no one can do these signs that You do unless God is with him."* **John 3:2**

Nicodemus receiving Jesus as *"...a teacher come from God..."* opened the door for supernatural revelation regarding secrets of the kingdom to be released to him. According to Jesus' words in **Matthew 10:40,** whenever anyone receives another disciple after the spirit, that person is not just receiving another disciple; he is actually receiving Christ and the Father who sent Christ. This action is a catalyst which serves to open the windows of heaven causing the supernatural to flow through the one being received to the one receiving. What an awesome principle!

I knew a minister personally who was called to the office of *"...prophet..."*. In a discussion regarding ministry one

Equipment of the Ministries

day this minister said every time he traveled to one particular local assembly the authority and anointing of the office of prophet would manifest. It was common knowledge the local assembly to which he was referring had altogether received this man as a prophet and every time he was scheduled to speak there they actually made advance preparations in faith to receive this man as a prophet. The moment this minister stepped up to the pulpit the people were receiving him as a prophet.

Coincidence or faith's application of a spiritual principle of the kingdom? *"...He who receives a prophet in the name of a prophet shall receive a prophet's reward...".* Could the name of a prophet simply be *"...prophet..."*? And, could the prophet's reward simply be the supernatural ministry provided through the office of prophet? We need to experience the benefit of this spiritual principle by exercising our faith to receive one another as spiritual men instead of mere men.

Consider James' writings regarding availing prayers.

> *"Is anyone among you suffering? Let him pray. Is anyone cheerful? Let him sing psalms. Is anyone among you sick? Let him call for the elders of the church, and let them pray over him, anointing him with oil in the name of the Lord. And the prayer of faith will save the sick, and the Lord will raise him up. And if he has committed sins, he will be forgiven. Confess your trespasses to one another, and pray for one another, that you may be healed. The effective, fervent prayer of a righteous man avails much. Elijah was a man with a nature like ours, and he prayed earnestly that it would not rain; and it did not rain on the land for three years and six months. And he prayed again, and the heaven gave rain, and the earth produced its fruit."* **James 5:13-18**

By inspiration from the Holy Spirit James is actually comparing the prayers of the saints with those of Elijah. He wrote *"...the effective fervent prayer of a righteous man avails much..."* and then immediately compared Elijah's prayers to those of the righteous. A significant reason the prayers of the saints do not avail more is because of the way we see ourselves as mere men instead of spiritual men. Many of the church on the earth today are captive to an insidious device of the enemy refusing to see themselves as righteous sons of God. Seeing ourselves as righteous spiritual men is a prerequisite to prayers that avail much. Our prayers as righteous men, righteous by the blood of the Lamb not our own goodness, are designed by God to produce supernatural results. This is the will of God! No wonder the enemy labors so diligently to keep his device in place to deceive as many as he can regarding how we see ourselves.

The Lord who gave these offices as gifts is also the One who has *"...vested..."* each office with certain equipment, revelation, and purpose. An illustration from the natural world will help leverage our understanding of *"...vesting..."* to the spiritual in these matters. Consider the offices of government for our nation. **Articles I, II,** and **III** of our **Constitution** describe the **legislative**, **executive**, and **judicial** branches of the federal government. These **Articles** establish the qualifications for each role, the manner of their election, their powers and limitations.

In times past in our nation's history when a President has been assassinated, even though the man holding the office was no longer alive, the office still remained very much

Equipment of the Ministries

"...alive..." with all of its powers and prestige. The powers of the presidency have been vested in the *"...office..."* rather than in the *"...man..."* holding the office.

If the office is vacated for any reason the powers of the office, although still vested in the office, are dormant. A person must be sworn into the office to have access to the powers of the office. The person sworn into the office, whether duly elected or by Constitutional order of succession, must learn the powers of the office and how to use them in order to successfully discharge the duties of the office.

No one becomes a powerful President solely on the basis on the talents, skills, or intellect he has as an individual. While all of these are necessary the office is just too large for it to be limited to the resources an individual can provide only as an individual to fulfill its duties. That is why the Constitution has vested powers in the *"...office...".* The President will use his talents, skills, and intellect to wield the powers vested in his office to be able to lead the nation.

In a parallel fashion persons called to one of the offices of ministry must know the office to which they have been called and learn the equipment, revelation, and purpose of the office and how to use them in order to be successful in that office. No individual believer could do what is necessary *"...to perfect the saints..."* by using only the resources he has as an individual. He needs the equipment of the office to successfully discharge the purpose of his office. Access to the equipment of any office is only possible to a person who is actually called by God to that particular office, identifies that calling, accepts it, and steps into the role of the office.

Making of a Ministry Gift

Although different men have held the exact same office of President, historical record declares some have been better Presidents than others. While there is certainly more than one variable involved in determining why one President was better than another, one particular variable is a priority, the extent to which the person sworn into the office understood and used the equipment of the office.

In the case of the office of President, the person sworn into the office not only needs to understand the equipment of the office and how to use it, but must also understand the office does not exist in a vacuum. That is, the office was established to be a part of a federal government made up of many parts, all parts required to work together to produce the desired results.

A term often used to describe the current political climate in our nation is *"...gridlocked..."*. This term was originally used to describe certain sections of city streets, *"...grids..."*, where traffic would come to a complete stop, with absolutely no movement. Application of this term to our current political situation seems very appropriate, especially when any part of the government sees itself in a vacuum.

Just like no political office exists in a vacuum, no office of ministry exists in a vacuum. All of the offices of ministry are designed by Christ to work together to produce the results Christ has ordained. All persons called to any of these offices of ministry do not stop being *"...flesh and bone parts of Christ's body..."* just because they are called to an office of ministry. All parts of a natural body must work together in order for that body to function properly and to fulfill its purpose in the natural world. If any of the parts of the body stop working together with the other parts, medical attention is required in order to address the malady and correct it if possible. All of the parts of a natural body are designed to work together for the good of the whole body *(See **I Corinthians 12:12-27**)*. This, too, is the pattern for the body of Christ. All parts are designed to work together for the good of the whole body.

Consider this natural illustration. The youth of a certain local assembly brought a fifty foot long telephone pole into the sanctuary as a prop for their ministry one weekend. At the conclusion of their time of ministry, they were so excited they forgot to remove the telephone pole before they left the sanctuary. That Sunday morning people began to ask about the pole. When it was determined how the telephone pole got there and that it was no longer needed, it was decided it needed to be removed.

Moving a fifty foot long telephone pole is no easy task no matter how strong you may be. In this scenario a number of people gathered at the telephone pole desiring to help move it out of the sanctuary. One person raised his hand in a gesture signifying halt and told the others, *"That's alright, I've got this."* How foolish! These foolish actions would be easily seen as a demonstration of some flaw in the character of the one involved in such absurdities. The greater the number of people willing and able to help move a fifty foot long telephone pole out of a building full of chairs, people, and Sunday morning *stuff* the better. The task is simply too great for any one person to accomplish alone.

So, too, the goal of ministry, *"...to reveal Christ to everyone so they may know Him to either be saved or grow to maturity..."*, is simply impossible for any one person. We should be encouraging everyone to be involved in the process. If we are not seeing such encouragement, the first place to look is our understanding of the purpose of all ministry. Do we understand how the fundamental building block of all ministry is to reveal Christ? If not, then, we need to receive and impart this revelation to all members of the body of Christ!!!

Because the responsibilities of each office are diverse and many, understanding the equipment the Lord has provided each office to fulfill their responsibilities is paramount for anyone called. The most important component of the equipment for our consideration is **the anointing**. It is essential for the church to understand the anointing. The relationship the church has with the anointing in the new covenant is vastly different from the relationship the people had with the anointing in the old covenant.

The anointing has been so mysterious, mystical, and illusive in our understanding it is almost non-practical. However, because it is such an important component of the equipment with which the Lord has equipped the offices of ministry, it is obligatory we have a simpler and clearer understanding. We must endeavor to demystify it, so those called to the ministry may be able to flow in it more efficiently. How well

Equipment of the Ministries

each person called to an office of ministry learns to relate to the anointing is going to determine the level of success that person has in ministry.

John considered the anointing an essential part of the lives of the believers to keep them from any negative influence from the many antichrists that were already present on the earth during the life and times of John the Beloved.

> "Little children, it is the last hour; and as you have heard that the Antichrist is coming, even now many antichrists have come, by which we know that it is the last hour. They went out from us, but they were not of us; for if they had been of us, they would have continued with us; but they went out that they might be made manifest, that none of them were of us. But **you have an anointing from the Holy One, and you know all things**. I have not written to you because you do not know the truth, but because you know it, and that no lie is of the truth. Who is a liar but he who denies that Jesus is the Christ? He is antichrist who denies the Father and the Son. Whoever denies the Son does not have the Father either; he who acknowledges the Son has the Father also."
> *I John 2:18-23*

> "**But the anointing which you have received from Him abides in you, and you do not need that anyone teach you; but as the same anointing teaches you concerning all things, and is true, and is not a lie, and just as it has taught you, you will abide in Him.**" *I John 2:27*

It would be advantageous for us to consider a natural world illustration to gain clear and simple understanding as a segue to considering the anointing. Verbal or written descriptions can serve to identify a person as much as a fingerprint or

Making of a Ministry Gift

DNA sampling. For example, one person is the Head of State, head of government of the United States, head of the executive branch of the federal government, and Commander-in-Chief of the United States Armed Forces. These descriptions or *"...fingerprints...."* can only identify one person: *the President of the United States*.

Using descriptions taken from Scripture, we can apply this same model to persons in the Bible. Our first Biblical illustration is the Lamb of God sent to take away the sin of the world, born of a virgin, was crucified dead and buried, and rose again the third day never to die again. These descriptions or *"...fingerprints..."* can only identify one person: *Jesus the Christ*.

John wrote a description in *I John 2:27* of something the believers had already received which is *"...in them, is true, and teaches them all things..."*. In John's gospel he recorded Jesus describing something the believers would receive as a gift from the Father who would *"...abide in them, be called the Spirit of Truth, and would teach them all things..."*. These descriptions in *I John 2:27* and the *fourteenth, fifteenth, and sixteenth chapters of John*, although using slightly different terms become *"...fingerprints..."* for the gift the believers were to receive. These fingerprints can only identify one person: *the Holy Spirit*.

Although the descriptions found in *I John 2:27* and *John, chapters 14, 15, and 16* all describe only one person, that one person is called by different names in the context of these various portions of Scripture: *"...The Holy Spirit, the Helper, the Spirit of Truth, and the Anointing..".* We know the *Holy Spirit* to be God, the Third Person of the Trinity. So, too, the *Helper*, the *Spirit of Truth*, and the *Anointing*, just different names for the same person, would be God also!

> ### God the Holy Spirit is the Anointing!

The person and ministry of the Holy Spirit was a mystery clothed in secrecy in the old covenant. When the fullness of time came for the new covenant, the Holy Spirit began to be revealed. When asked by His disciples why He taught the people in parables, Jesus told them it was because of the condition of their heart *(Matthew 13:10-17)*. In this same context He said, however, *"...it is given to you to know the mysteries of the kingdom of heaven..." **Matthew 13:11**.* By the end of Jesus' earthly ministry, He was speaking plainly to His most intimate disciples about the Holy Spirit.

People had a vastly different relationship with the Holy Spirit in the old covenant. Jesus' earthly ministry represented a transition between the old covenant and the new covenant. In a discussion with His disciples regarding the giving of the Holy Spirit as a gift from the Father as a provision of the new covenant, He told them their relationship with the Holy Spirit would change after He went away. He said...

> *"...you know Him, for He dwells with you and will be in you..."* **John 14:16**

The difference between an external relationship with the Holy Spirit and an internal relationship is beyond compare! An abiding internal relationship with God the Holy Spirit is truly a supernatural provision from our loving Father!

This internal abiding presence of the Holy Spirit defines the type of relationship we are to have with the Holy Spirit in the new covenant, whether minister or non-minister. While there are Scripture references from the Old Testament and the New Testament about the Holy Spirit coming upon a person, there is clearly a change between the old covenant relationship people had with the Holy Spirit and the new covenant.

Consider Samuel's Old Testament account of the Holy Spirit coming upon Saul shortly after Saul had been anointed to be King. Samuel is prophesying to Saul...

> *"...After that you shall come to the hill of God where the Philistine garrison is. And it will happen, when you have come there to the city, that you will meet a group of prophets coming down from the high place with a stringed instrument, a tambourine, a flute, and a harp before them; and they will be prophesying. Then the **Spirit of the Lord will come upon you, and you will prophesy with them and be turned into another man...***"
> *I Samuel 10:5,6*

Jesus experienced the Holy Spirit coming upon Him in the New Testament. Just as Jesus was coming up from the water when He was being baptized by John, John said he saw, *"...**the Spirit of God descending like a dove and alighting upon Him**...*"

Equipment of the Ministries

(Matthew 3:16). Jesus provides us with another illustration of an external manifestation of the Holy Spirit in His life. One Sabbath in the synagogue He took the book of the prophet Isaiah and found the place where it is written,

> "...*the Spirit of the Lord is upon Me*, because He has anointed Me...closed the book...and began to say to them, 'Today this Scripture is fulfilled in your hearing...'
> **Luke 4:17-21**

Even the disciples had a similar encounter, where the Holy Spirit came upon them.

> "When the Day of Pentecost had fully come, they were all with one accord in one place. And suddenly there came a sound from heaven, as of a rushing mighty wind, and it filled the whole house where they were sitting. Then there appeared to them divided tongues, as of fire, and **one sat upon each of them. And they were all filled with the Holy Spirit** and began to speak with other tongues, as the Spirit gave them utterance." **Acts 2:1-4**

There are other New Testament Scripture references talking about the Holy Spirit coming upon people primarily at the time of their first encounter with the Holy Spirit.

However, when Jesus was giving His eleven most intimate disciples understanding about the Holy Spirit and His future ministries to the disciples in *chapters fourteen, fifteen, and sixteen of John,* He began His discussion by saying, *"...He dwells with you and **will be in you**..." (John 14:17)*. We can conclude from Jesus' words of instruction to His disciples regarding the Holy Spirit that the basis for our relationship with the Holy Spirit in the new covenant is primarily internal. We must not discount any external manifestation the Holy Spirit provides in our lives, however, our attention needs to focus on the internal. This is the new covenant parameter around which we need to develop our skills.

Another extremely significant understanding needs to be established regarding the Holy Spirit. While there are a diversity of manifestations of the Holy Spirit, there is only One Holy Spirit. Because the Holy Spirit is the Anointing, this same understanding applies. There are a diversity of manifestations of the Anointing, but there is only One Anointing. He is God the Holy Spirit the Anointing!

The Holy Spirit as the Anointing will provide each minister standing in each office of ministry the abilities to fulfill their roles as ministers. To say there is an apostolic anointing, a prophetic anointing, an evangelistic anointing, a pastoral anointing, and a teaching anointing tends to lead the hearer astray. There is only One Anointing who will provide diverse manifestations to all of the offices of ministry according to the function of each office. Our goal is to make our relationship with the Holy Spirit as the Anointing as efficient and practical as possible. Developing one relationship with one Holy Spirit who is also the Anointing is easier than trying to decipher a wide array of anointing and having to learn to walk in all of them. Just learn to be intimate with the Holy Spirit as the Anointing, and He will provide you with whatever is necessary, after all He is God as much as the Father and the Son!

Equipment of the Ministries

Shifting our considerations from old covenant understandings of the anointing to new covenant simplifies our options for developing a connection with the anointing. Because the Anointing is a person who is God, our priority is to develop a *"...relationship..."* with the Anointing.

As we have considered Jesus' words regarding how we obtain life like God has it a number of times and will continue to consider them over and over again, we consider them once again here. Jesus has presented us with a profound spiritual principle which will produce rich dividends in our lives if we understand it and walk in the light of it.

> *"And this is eternal life, that they may know You, the only true God, and Jesus Christ whom You have sent."*
> **John 17:3**

Jesus is telling us the quality of life we have will be proportionate to the knowledge of the Father and the Son we have. ***Knowing God produces life!*** It is easy to apply our faith to believe that knowing God the Holy Spirit will produce the same proportionate result. This surely is the plan and will of God, that we grow in the knowledge of our God: Father, Son, and Holy Spirit!

Because Jesus is the pattern for our lives, we need to know His way as the example for the way we are to live. Luke recorded some special events in the life of Jesus just after Jesus was baptized in the River Jordan and just after John saw the Holy Spirit descending in bodily form like a dove upon Him *(Luke 3:21,22)*:

Making of a Ministry Gift

> *"Then Jesus, being **filled with the Holy Spirit**, returned from the Jordan and was **led by the Spirit** into the wilderness, being tempted for forty days by the devil..."*
> **Luke 4:1,2**

> *"Then Jesus returned in the power of the Spirit to Galilee, and news of Him went out through all the surrounding region. And He taught in their synagogues, being glorified by all. So He came to Nazareth, where He had been brought up. And as His custom was, He went into the synagogue on the Sabbath day, and stood up to read. And He was handed the book of the prophet Isaiah. And when He had opened the book, He found the place where it was written:*
>
>> *'**The Spirit of the Lord is upon Me, because He has anointed** Me to preach the gospel to the poor; He has sent Me to heal the brokenhearted, to proclaim liberty to the captives and recovery of sight to the blind, to set at liberty those who are oppressed; to proclaim the acceptable year of the Lord. Then He closed the book, and gave it back to the attendant and sat down. And the eyes of all who were in the synagogue were fixed on Him. And He began to say to them, 'Today this Scripture is fulfilled in your hearing.'* **Luke 4:14-21**

Three really significant pieces of revelation are presented in these few verses of Scripture about Jesus and the Holy Spirit.

1. **Jesus was filled with the Holy Spirit.**
2. **Jesus was led by the Spirit.**
3. **Jesus was anointed by the Spirit of the Lord.**

Equipment of the Ministries

This is to be the pattern for our lives and ministries. We are to be *"...filled with the Holy Spirit..."*, *"...led by the Spirit..."*, and *"...anointed by the Spirit of the Lord..."*. The Spirit of the Lord anointed Jesus *"...to preach the gospel to the poor; ...to heal the brokenhearted, to proclaim liberty to the captives and recovery of sight to the blind, to set at liberty those who are oppressed; to proclaim the acceptable year of the Lord."*. In other words, the Holy Spirit provided the ability for Jesus to fulfill all of these ministries. There wasn't an anointing to preach the gospel to the poor, and another anointing to heal the brokenhearted, and another, and another... There was one Anointing who was *"...the ability of God..."* for Jesus to be able to do whatever God willed for Him to do.

God the Holy Spirit, the Anointing, is *"...the ability of God..."* for us to be able to do whatever God wills for us to do. While there will surely be many diverse activities for each ministry requiring the ability of God, there are three ministerial functions common to all offices of ministry for which *"...the ability of God..."* is required.

1. The first is the ability to **procure and understand the revelation of Christ** appropriate to each office to which we are called.

2. The second is the ability to **impart that revelation** to the saints.

3. The third is the ability **to *"...see..."* beyond the sight of a non-ministry individual believer**. All offices of ministry must be able to *"...see the big picture..."* in some measure. They must be able to see what has al-

ready been *"...built..."* within the saints so they will be able to build accurately upon it *(I Corinthians 3:10)*. They also must be able to see whether the saints are doing the word in order to steward the revelation which has been given.

> *God as the Anointing!*
> *What a magnificent piece of Equipment*
> *through which all ministries fulfill their roles!*

Chapter Four

Stewardship

The apostle Paul was a man of great passion for God. In the first part of his life he was a scholar full of zeal for what he believed to be the truth regarding God even though it was not according to the knowledge of Christ. Although Scripture told us God separated him from his mother's womb to preach Christ, it was not until later in his life, in his encounter with the Lord on the Damascus Road, that he came to the knowledge of Jesus the Christ.

> *"...it pleased God, who separated me (Paul) from my mother's womb and called me through His grace, to reveal His Son in me, that I might preach Him among the Gentiles, I did not immediately confer with flesh and blood, nor did I go up to Jerusalem to those who were apostles before me; but I went to Arabia, and returned again to Damascus..."* **Galatians 1:15-17**

Once he had embraced Jesus to be his Lord and accepted his calling to the ministry, he transferred his passion, zeal, and scholarly approach to life directly to his relationship with the Christ and the church. Paul's life and ministry serve as wonderful examples for all of us to admire and aspire to be as passionate, zealous, and scholarly.

Paul wrote about the subject of *"...stewardship..."* in letters to the church at Corinth and the church at Colosse. In the letter to the church at Corinth while writing about stewardship, he opened the door to an extremely significant revelation necessary for all who are called to the ministry: *"...being **servants** of Christ..."*. Before we can consider *"...stewardship..."*, we must attempt to understand ministers *"...as servants of Christ..."*.

> *"Let a man so consider us, as **servants** (5257) of Christ and stewards (3623) of the mysteries of God. Moreover it is required in stewards that one be found faithful..."*
> **I Corinthians 4:1,2**
>
> *5257 **huperetes** from 5259* and a der. of *eresso* (to *row*); an *under-oarsman*, i.e. (gen.) *subordinate* (*assistant, sexton, constable*): -- minister, officer, servant.

Paul's declaration that ministers were *"...servants of Christ..."* does not undermine ministers' roles as *"...sons of God..."*. Every person birthed into the kingdom of God was redeemed to be a son of God. No one was redeemed just to be a servant. Nothing can change that truth! The role of minister is a subsequent role to a person's role as son. Sonship is the foundation for all roles in the church including minister.

No matter to which role a person may be called after new birth, all roles must sit on the foundation of the role of **believer**. We have already stated, *"...All persons called to any of these offices of ministry do not stop being "...flesh and bone parts of Christ's body..." just because they are called to an office of ministry..."*. The enemy desires to steal the life of the word from us. His first approach is to try to steal the word that has been sown into peoples' heart. If he cannot do that he sows subtle seeds of deception in an effort to corrupt the truth.

Stewardship

The role of ministry is just such a revelation he has attacked. If he can alter our understanding just a little, he can greatly hinder the purpose of the ministries.

His devices have taken on many forms, but one of his favorites seems to be to use the truth we have received and try to corrupt it. One such truth was written by Paul about himself but is relevant to all called to the ministry. Paul wrote *"...God has separated me from my mother's womb to preach Christ...".* The device the enemy uses here is to make it seem as if the separation *to* an office of ministry is separating the person *from* the body of Christ.

God's calling separates a person within the body of Christ to an office of ministry, not from the body of Christ to an office of ministry. The difference between these two notions is the difference between ministers serving the sons of God to ministers being served by the sons of God. We are to honor and respect those called to offices of ministry but as joint heirs with one another and with Christ as parts of the same body, not as beyond approach because of their calling.

> *"...those members of the body which seem to be weaker are necessary. And those members of the body which we think to be less honorable, on these we bestow greater honor; and our unpresentable parts have greater modesty, but our presentable parts have no need. But God composed the body, having given greater honor to that part which lacks it, that there should be no schism in the body, but that the members should have the same care for one another. And **if one member suffers, all the members suffer with it; or if one member is honored, all the members rejoice with it. Now you are the body of Christ and members individually...*" *I Corinthians 12:22-27*

Making of a Ministry Gift

Anytime any minister assumes a posture greater than the ones to whom he is sent, a corruption is at work. Anytime any believer assigns an honor to any minister greater than the honor associated with being a son of God, a corruption is at work. All ministry must be set on the foundation of life as believers. There is no greater honor than being a joint heir with Christ as the Seed of Abraham, a son of God!

We have already stated, *"...**the fundamental building block of all ministry** no matter who does the work thereof...**is to reveal Christ...**"* As ministers serve the Lord Christ and the church, we all still walk together as one body. To make sure we remain on the foundation of revealing Christ as the fundamental building block of all ministry, our roles as ministers must be established on our knowledge of sonship and our maturity as sons.

Once I experienced first-hand how a minister can be honored to be seemingly greater than a son of God. I was in a foreign nation many years ago. I had been up-country in a remote region of the nation for weeks. A minister friend and I were on this trip together, so we could travel and minister as a team. Our flight out of the country back to the USA only departed from one of the major cities in the nation. Travel arrangements in remote foreign places are not always efficient, so we arrived in the major city the day before we were scheduled to depart. We decided to attend a church service while waiting.

Stewardship

An American minister of great experience and reputation was scheduled to speak that morning. We were thinking we would have a kindred spirit with this man since the three of us were fellow Americans ministering in this foreign land. After the service we were going to ask him to pray for us because we were very drained from so long a time of ministering up country. As we were walking down one of the main hallways in the church building to get to the minister, we saw him coming straight toward us down the same hallway. We were both delighted, thinking this was the provision of the Lord.

As we got closer we could see the people walking near this man were not just walking near him, they were surrounding him as secret service agents would surround the President. It seemed strange since their group and the two of us were the only ones in the hallway. When we reached the group, I reached out my hand to greet the minister and to ask for him to pray for us. One of the men walking in the group brushed my hand aside, and they all kept walking. There were no verbal exchanges, only the brushing of my hand aside.

The minister traveling with me and I posed no threat; we did not look menacing. We were exhausted and in need of prayer. Even if this minister would have been as exhausted as we were, we could have all prayed together and helped strengthen one another. I must confess my attitude was not stellar or even spiritual those many years ago. I have grown in understanding and maturity since then. I use this illustration only because it so spectacularly demonstrates our subject matter.

Making of a Ministry Gift

In his letter to the church at Colosse, Paul continued with this very important subject of *"...stewardship..."*.

> *"I now rejoice in my sufferings for you, and fill up in my flesh what is lacking in the afflictions of Christ, for the sake of His body, which is the church, of which I became a minister according to the* **stewardship (3622)** *from God which was given to me for you, to fulfill the word of God, the mystery which has been hidden from ages and from generations, but now has been revealed to His saints. To them God willed to make known what are the riches of the glory of this mystery among the Gentiles: which is Christ in you, the hope of glory. Him we preach, warning every man and teaching every man in all wisdom, that we may present every man perfect in Christ. To this end I also labor, striving according to His working which works in me mightily."* **Colossians 1:24-29**

3622 oikonomia from *3623*; *administration* (of a household or estate); spec. a (religious) *"economy"*: -- dispensation, stewardship.

3623 oikonomos from *3624* and the base of *3551*; a *house-distributor* (i.e. *manager*), or *overseer*, i.e. an employee in that capacity; by extens. a fiscal *agent* (*treasurer*); fig. a *preacher* (of the Gospel): -- chamberlain, governor, steward.

Strong's Exhaustive Concordance of the Bible

stewardship - the position, duties, or service of a steward.

steward - a man entrusted with the management of the household or estate of another; one employed to manage the domestic affairs, superintend the servants, collect the rents or income, keep the accounts.

Webster's New Universal Unabridged Dictionary

Stewardship

Paul writes the ministries are **stewards** of the mysteries of God. In other words, ministers are responsible to steward the revelation they have received. ***How does stewarding the mysteries of God work?*** Notice Paul said the ministers were the stewards of the mysteries of God. He did not say God would steward the mysteries. In other words, in order for all ministers to be found faithful as stewards they must be the ones who actually do the stewarding of the mysteries they have been given. ***What does that stewarding look like?***

In the natural world when a man is entrusted with the role of steward for an estate, there is no pretense that right of ownership of *"...the affairs, servants, rents or income, or accounts..."* is to be transferred to the steward. The steward is simply the person to whom the rightful owner has chosen to entrust the oversight of all these things. In this natural world example the steward, even though not the owner, is responsible for the collection and disbursement of finances, to direct the servants, and to keep the accounts. At the time the man is appointed to be steward he is provided the necessary information regarding the estate so he can fulfill his role.

Consider the role of a college professor. Generally, a professor on staff at a university is there to *"...teach..."* a particular subject. The course for which the professor is responsible has a beginning and an ending, typically one semester. The role of steward applies to the professor in relation to the course he is to teach. He must carefully dispense the content of his material over the appropriate number of hours, days, weeks, and months of the semester. He must also be con-

Making of a Ministry Gift

stantly aware of how well the students are assimilating the materials before he can expect to successfully introduce new materials. The role of steward is the professor's, not the university's.

The role of accountant in a business is another natural world illustration requiring stewardship. The accountant is typically responsible for accounts receivable and accounts payable. Accounts payable require stewarding in a very specific manner. Whether rent, utilities, mortgage, payroll, or other regularly paid items the accountant must disburse the proper amount to the proper person at the proper time. For example, the electric company sends the business a monthly statement with a specified amount due and a due date. The accountant, as the steward for the business, is responsible to pay the exact amount due on or before the due date in order for the business to continue enjoying the benefits of the electricity supplied by the electric company. If the electricity is cut off, one of the first places management will look is to the accountant to see if he did his part. The accountant is the steward for the business.

How do the illustrations of the steward of an estate, the college professor, and the business accountant apply to the offices of ministry as stewards? Stewardship operates principally, exactly the same for the steward of an estate, the college professor, the business accountant, or the ministries. There is no pretense in the understanding of the ministries who is rightful of owner of the people. Ministries know the design for the operation and ultimate goal of the church is God's.

Stewardship

The offices of ministry have been given the task of perfecting the saints by imparting revelation of Christ specific and unique to each of their offices so the saints may grow in that knowledge to maturity, to the measure of the stature of the fullness of Christ.

The ministers are each given a specific and unique revelation of Christ. That revelation is given to them to be a part of the whole revelation of Christ together with the other offices of ministry. The revelation each office receives *"...fits..."* together with other revelation. Minister's stewarding responsibilities are comprised of *primarily* three parts:

1. **Ministering appropriate revelation to the saints.**
2. **Monitoring the progress of the saints.**
3. **Building on the revelation already given to the saints.**

The first of these two stewarding parts, **"...ministering appropriate revelation to the saints..."** is easily seen in Peter's first epistle. Peter, writing to those who were newly born again, declared the appropriate revelation for the saints was *"...the pure milk of the word...".*

> *"...as newborn babes, desire the pure milk of the word, that you may grow thereby..."* **I Peter 2:2**

Throughout the New Testament the writers often compared natural to spiritual in relation to our lives in the kingdom. Here Peter uses just such a comparison calling those who are new believers *"...newborn babes...".* He draws on the common knowledge everyone has of the natural newborn who requires milk to be nourished in order to grow, instructing the newborn babes in Christ to desire the pure milk of the word that they may grow.

John used this same type of natural world comparison when he wrote in his first epistle about various levels of spiritual growth using such terms as: *"...little children, young men, and fathers...".* The author of the letter to the Hebrew Christians considered *"...diet-appropriate..."* revelation based on spiritual development: milk for babes, solid food for the more skilled.

> *"...you have come to need milk and not solid food. For everyone who partakes only of milk is unskilled in the word of righteousness, for he is a babe. But solid food belongs to those who by reason of use have their senses exercised to discern both good and evil..."*
> **Hebrews 5:12-14**

In order for the ministers to effectively steward the revelation they have each received regarding revelation needed by each growth level of the saints, they must be able to identify revelation as either milk or solid food. No matter how wonderful *"...solid food revelation..."* is to a person capable of partaking of it, scripture teaches it is not for a babe in Christ who is only able to partake of the *"...milk of the word...".* The responsibility to steward the revelation needed for each growth level is the ministers', not the saint's, and not God's.

The writer of the letter to the Hebrew Christians also addresses the second stewarding part, **"...*monitoring the progress of the saints...*":** *"...For though by this time you ought to*

Stewardship

be teachers, you need someone to teach you again the first principles of the oracles of God...". Food appropriate for each level of development for natural children provides the nutritional components necessary for children to grow. Of course, their growth is not exclusively a result of the food they eat. They must also have ample exercise and rest. In the natural world if a newborn stops being hungry, this condition is typically symptomatic of some infirmity. Unless the infirmity can be diagnosed and treated, the child will suffer dire consequences. In this natural world illustration the parents are the stewards of the child. They must monitor the child's progress.

The easy order of life for a newborn is eat, sleep, exercise, and grow. There are few changes to this order throughout the course of a childhood. The child's parents must continually monitor their child through the stages of growth to make sure all of these components for growth are present. If any one of them is lacking or over-provided, the child will suffer. The parents are the stewards to make sure all of these components remain adequate in the child's life. This parent-child model was surely the design of God.

In a parallel fashion the children of God must be monitored in order to be provided the greatest opportunity for success. The ministers are the foundation for this monitoring process, however, it is clear it is not likely for there to be a one to one ratio of ministers to saints. Therefore, God must have provision for the children of God to be monitored. The letter to the Hebrew Christians stating, *"...For though by this time you ought to be teachers..."* provides us with direction to find answers in this matter.

Making of a Ministry Gift

This letter is written to the entire church. Certainly, all members of the church were not called to the *office of teacher*, so *"...you ought to be teachers..."* must have an alternative meaning. This declaration *"...you ought to be teachers..."* is merely admonishing the members of the church to freely give what they have freely received: one believer helping another believer. This is the pattern of the natural family: older siblings helping younger siblings.

Scripture clearly teaches that a person who hears the word only and is not a doer deceives himself *(James 1:21-25)*. The stewardship part which monitors the progress of the saints will help to prevent the saints from being hearers only. The ministers' roles as stewards in this matter only give opportunity for the saints not to be hearers only. Their stewardship roles do not give the ministers any *"...control..."* over the saints, only *"...help..."*! If the saints choose to be hearers only, their decision must be honored, but the ministers need to make it clear to the saints their choice will result in self-deception.

Paul's letter to the church at Corinth discusses the third stewarding part, ***"...building on the revelation already given to the saints...".*** Paul was addressing the carnal conflict which existed among the church involving division based on individual believer's identification with various ministers. The Corinthians were seeing only as mere men causing them to see the ministers who had ministered to them incorrectly. It was in this context that Paul also addressed the relationship ministers are to have with one another.

Stewardship

> *"Who then is Paul, and who is Apollos, but ministers through whom you believed, as the Lord gave to each one? I planted, Apollos watered, but God gave the increase. So then neither he who plants is anything, nor he who waters, but God who gives the increase. Now he who plants and he who waters are one, and each one will receive his own reward according to his own labor. For we are God's fellow workers; you are God's field, you are God's building. According to the grace of God which was given to me, as a wise master builder I have laid the foundation, and another builds on it. But let each one take heed how he builds on it..."*
> *I Corinthians 3:5-10*

Paul writes of the church using two different natural illustrations, *"...you are God's field, you are God's building..."*. He then writes of himself, *"...as a wise master builder I have laid the foundation, and another builds on it. But let each one take heed how he builds on it..."*. Using *"...you are God's building..."* to begin to understand the building concept within the church opens the door for us to use a natural world comparison to better understand the relationship between builders.

Building a natural building involving a number of different builders requires each of the builders to build on what has already been completed in the building process. For example, the roofers can only build the roof if the prerequisite construction has already been completed. The roof cannot be constructed prior to prerequisite construction simply because there is a great need for the roof *(such as if it is raining)*. There are many such illustrations involved in building a natural building.

Making of a Ministry Gift

Using Paul's illustration of the church as *"...God's building..."* and himself as a *"...wise master builder..."*, we can easily use this same comparative illustration to consider the other offices of ministry. Each of the ministers must work in harmony in order to see *"...God's building..."* completed. In principle, neither a natural nor a spiritual building can be completed without building on what has already been built. Of course this illustration, as does every illustration, breaks down somewhere. One of the builders has to start the entire building process: Such as excavating the construction site.

With further exploration of this concept of building on what has already been built, we can use specific ministry illustrations to promote a more practical understanding. The office of apostle is a foundation laying ministry. One of the foundation stones is *"...faith toward God..."*. According to the writer of the letter to the Hebrew Christians, the basic principles of the doctrine of Christ are all foundational revelation. As such, that means the revelation of *"...faith toward God..."* ministered as one of the basic principles of the doctrine of Christ is only a foundational part of the revelation of faith needed by the saints. Another layer of the revelation of faith is designed to be *"...built..."* on this basic understanding of faith so the saints can continue to grow in their knowledge and subsequent skills of faith.

The basic principle of faith is primarily oriented to helping believers establish their relationship with our God.

> *"Without faith it is impossible to please Him, for he who comes to God must believe that He is, and that He is a rewarder of those who diligently seek Him."*
>   *Hebrews 11:6*

Stewardship

The pleasure a believer brings to God by having faith is not the amount of faith the believer has nor the performance of that faith to do great exploits, but rather the simple fact that the believer has used the faith God has given him as the means to be born again. It pleases our God for us to be saved from death and to partake of eternal life. A performance based value system is a dangerous place for the sons of God to go or to be taken. Truly what we do is of great value to our God, but our value is determined on the basis of who we are!

Suppose a little child grows up under the oversight of a *"...perfectionist..."* father. Such a condition will cause the little child to feel like he never measures up but is having to always try harder in order to *"...please..."* his father. This form of life is very destructive for the little child! The love and acceptance from the father, whether overtly stated or just implied, seems to be inextricably linked to the little child's performance. ***Abba is not like this!*** He desires to establish our relationship on the basis of His love for us.

While our performance has great bearing on the quality of life we live, it does not alter God's love for us. God's love is precisely the reason He so diligently labors with us to give us opportunities to grow in our knowledge of Him so we can partake of greater levels of life like He has it. For example,

> *"Do you not know that to whom you present yourselves slaves to obey, you are that one's slaves whom you obey, whether of sin leading to death, or of obedience leading to righteousness?"* **Romans 6:16**

Making of a Ministry Gift

God the Holy Spirit did not inspire Paul to write this and the associated verses comprising all of *chapters five, six, seven, and eight of Romans* as the means of instilling in us the notion that if we sin, God will be mad at us or no longer love us. Quite the contrary! God the Holy Spirit inspired Paul to write this letter to show us the danger of sin and how much Abba desires to help us avoid it and all of its consequences.

If a believer is taught that God loves him no matter what he does without also being taught that what he does has great bearing on the quality of life he lives, he will easily fall victim to one of the enemy's devices. Love and performance are not **either or**, they are, *"...God loves me for who I am..."*, **and** *"...God cares about my performance because it has great bearing on the quality of life I live..."!* The basic principle of *faith* provides believers this simple yet profound understanding of our relationship with our God.

Once believers have an accurate understanding of the basis of God's relationship with us and how faith establishes our connection, then we can begin to build on this revelation of *faith*. I remember when the importance of the revelation of faith began to emerge in the church. No matter what the ministers who taught faith intended, many in the church took the concept of faith and inappropriately applied it. Instead of applying faith to establish an intimate relationship with our God, many began to apply their faith to appropriate all the things the Gentiles seek. In retrospect it appears the saints simply did not have the basic principle of faith or were not walking in it before another layer of faith began to be given to them.

Stewardship

Matthew recorded the words of Jesus telling us to *"...seek first the kingdom..." **(Matthew 6:24-34)***. Jesus was not telling us ***not*** to seek the things the Gentiles seek, only to seek them in the proper order. Anytime anyone seeks the things the Gentiles seek as their priority, they are opposing the commandment of the Lord who told us very plainly to "...seek ***first*** the kingdom...".

Perhaps the church at Laodicea faltered in their faith as a result of just such a misstep. They achieved the wealth of the natural world in such measures that Jesus said of them, *"...you say, I am rich, have become wealthy, and have need of nothing...".* It is clear, using Jesus' assessment, they had lost the practical application of their faith to establish and continue relationship with our God. Their priorities were out of order.

If believers in any local assembly return to a mere man form of life, stewardship requires the ministers with whom these believers are connected to identify their mere man condition and to give them opportunity to repent and return to life as spiritual people. A profoundly important truth is required to be constantly in play with every person called to any office of ministry: A carnal person whose heart is not willing to turn toward the Lord cannot be reached! As ministers called by God we must be constantly aware our God has given us the supernatural equipment necessary to fulfill our ministries, but this equipment will only work for a people who are willing to receive us as men sent by God, the same way it worked for Jesus *(Matthew 10:40-42)!* He is the pattern we are to follow.

Making of a Ministry Gift

Chapter Five

Another Gospel

The legendary singer songwriter Bob Dylan wrote a song in 1965 entitled **Highway 61**. In 2004 the song was ranked as one of the top 500 songs ever written. The first verse of the song references the Biblical account of God instructing Abraham to offer Isaac on the altar *(Genesis 22:1-8)*.

Oh, God said to Abraham, "Kill me a son"
Abe says, "Man you must be puttin' me on"
God says, "No", Abe say "What?"
God say "You can do what you want Abe but
The next time you see me comin' you better run"

Well Abe said, "Where do you want this killin' done?"
God say, "Out on Highway 61"

While the song has been sung by a number of artists since its writing, perhaps it became most well known when sung by Johnny Cash in two popular movies; **The Hunted** in 2003 and **Walk The Line** in 2005.

Abraham offering his son Isaac as a sacrifice serves as a precursor to God offering His only begotten son as the sacrifice for all mankind. Did you ever actually think about what it took to redeem you? The Triune God conceived of a plan requiring the second part of the Trinity to be clothed in flesh, to be made in the likeness of man, to be born of a virgin, to live a sin free life while on earth *(something no other man had ever been able to do)*, to be crucified, dead, and buried, to be

Making of a Ministry Gift

raised again from the dead after three days of death, all to be the spotless Lamb of God to take away the sin of the world.

In order for a lost person of the world to be saved, he must as a very minimum believe Jesus was crucified, dead, and buried and raised from the dead as the sacrificial provision required to take away his sin.

> *"...if you confess with your mouth the Lord Jesus and believe in your heart that God has raised Him from the dead, you will be saved..."* **Romans 10:9**

In most church meetings, especially directed toward evangelism, the subject matter of incarnation, Jesus born of a virgin, Jesus the Lamb of God sent to take away the sin of the world, Jesus crucified dead and buried, Jesus being raised from the dead on the third day partaking of eternal life never to die again are all presented in one form or another.

The church asks the lost people of the world not only to accept all of these things but to believe them. How is that possible? How can the church expect people of the world to believe these things? How can lost people believe any of these things? Any one of these things alone is beyond belief in this natural world! Man in his own natural ability cannot believe any of these things! God not only conceived the plan to redeem mankind, but He also made a way for man to believe in order to partake of His plan.

> *"Oh foolish Galatians! Who has bewitched you that you should not obey the truth, before whose eyes Jesus Christ was clearly portrayed among you as crucified? This only*

Another Gospel

I want to learn from you: Did you receive the Spirit by the works of the law, or by the hearing of faith? Are you so foolish? Having begun in the Spirit, are you now being made perfect by the flesh? Have you suffered so many things in vain -- if indeed it was in vain? Therefore He who supplies the Spirit to you and works miracles among you, does He do it by the works of the law, or by the hearing of faith? -- just as Abraham 'believed God, and it was accounted to him for righteousness.' Therefore know that only those who are of faith are sons of Abraham. And the Scripture, forseeing that God would justify the Gentiles by faith, preached the gospel to Abraham beforehand, saying 'In you all the nations shall be blessed.' So then those who are of faith are blessed with believing Abraham." **Galatians 3:1-9**

"For by grace you have been saved through faith, and that not of yourselves; it is the gift of God, not of works, lest anyone should boast." **Ephesians 2:8**

With man it is impossible to believe any of the things about Jesus regarding salvation, but God made a way for man to be able to believe. In fact, God's way sets the stage for the entire new covenant. The old covenant did not produce the results God desired because it was based on man's ability. The new covenant was designed and established on better promises. These better promises revolve around man being able to participate in the new covenant exclusively in the ability God provides. Man, lost or otherwise, can only believe and receive the things of the new covenant in the ability of God.

Consider the term *"...gospel..." (2097)*.

2097 euaggelizo from *2095* and *32*; *to announce good news* ("evangelize") espec. the gospel: -- declare, bring (declare, show) glad (good) tidings, preach (the gospel).

Making of a Ministry Gift

Strong's Exhaustive Concordance of the Bible

The *"...good news..."* is not only the revelation of Jesus as the Lamb of God given to take away the sin of the world, but also that God has designed the new covenant to be based on the ability He has provided mankind. Man no longer has to attempt to do the will of God in his own ability. God has provided His ability as the means for man doing His will! All man has to do is receive God's way as a free gift and walk in the power of it. Now, that is good news, the true gospel!

The enemy seems to always be laboring with his subtle devices to deceive the church by sowing seeds of corruption into the church. Paul's question to the church at Galatia ought to raise a huge red flag among us: *"...Who has bewitched you?..."*. We must be constantly on guard to keep from being bewitched.

> *"Be sober, be vigilant; because your adversary the devil walks about like a roaring lion, seeking whom he may devour. Resist him steadfast in the faith, knowing that the same sufferings are experienced by your brotherhood in the world."* Peter 5:8,9

The gospel is Jesus as the means of salvation and faith as the ability God has given us to partake of that salvation. This is the good news. Any time any *different* news comes to us regarding salvation or the way of the new covenant, that news can surely be seen as an effort of the enemy to corrupt the gospel we have already received into becoming *"...another gospel..."*. The devices of the enemy typically are not given in an effort to cause us to accept a completely different gospel. Instead they seem to be designed more subtly as seeds of deception sown in an effort to cause us to embrace a tiny little change in the gospel we have already received. Something so innocent looking and sounding it just seems right, such as how *"...hard..."* it is to believe the things of the kingdom. No! Absolutely not! This is the first stage of the enemy's effort to deceive us. It is not *"...hard..."* to believe the things of the kingdom; it is *"...impossible..."*!!! Natural man simply cannot believe any of the things required for salvation in his own ability. They are naturally *"...impossible..."* to believe! But, God has made a way, His way. That way is for us to be able to believe with the free gift He provides: *"...faith...".* God's way will not allow man to be able to boast in anything except God.

I have discussed a certain topic with many ministers over the years, but one particular conversation demonstrates the subtlety of a traditional trap best of all. I was engaged in a conversation with two other ministers about a specific office of ministry. One of them believed he was called to this specific ministry which was different from the ministry in which he had been representing himself for years. He was in transition to begin ministering in what he believed to be his true ministry. The third minister counseled him not to tell the churches to whom he would be invited his true ministry because they would not be able to receive it right now. I asked what he meant. He replied the church was just not able to receive the title of the office to which the second minister believed himself to be called. I pressed, *"The lost of the world are asked to receive Jesus as born of a virgin, crucified dead and buried, raised from the dead, bore all the sins of the world on Himself as the means of providing salvation to us, but the church who has been born again and has received God the Holy Spirit as our teacher cannot receive the title of an office of ministry given by Christ as one of the gifts necessary to perfect us?"* The third minister replied, *"They're not the same."*

Another illustration, this time from the natural world, will serve us well here. Whether true or not I cannot say, but the content of this story I believe represents an accurate principle. An experiment was conducted in a school system. Students from a special ed class were assigned to the teacher for the gifted, and the gifted students were assigned to the special ed teacher. Neither teacher knew of this experiment. Each teacher was told the students they had been assigned were the appropriate students they had been hired to teach. Each teacher began to teach their students accordingly. The gifted students in the special ed class began to function below their scholastic aptitude while the special ed students in the gifted class began to excel.

Whether this illustration is true or not is not really important because it parallels a simliar, although a spiritual principle, set down by Jesus in **Matthew 10:40-42**: *"...The way we receive one another determines the result of our enounter..."*. If a minister looks at the members of a local assembly as if they are not able to receive revelation from God because it is just too *"...hard..."* to receive, the minister with such a belief is not seeing correctly. The only reason not to give believers a revelation from God is because it does not conform to their level of spiritual growth, not because it is just too *"...hard..."*

for them to receive. Now is the time for the sons of God to learn of the offices of ministry the Lord Himself has given to perfect us. Now is the time for the sons of God to learn how to receive and relate to apostles, prophets, evangelists, pastors, and teachers.

Imagine traveling to a distant foreign land expressly for the purpose of ministering Christ to a lost people and starting a local assembly comprised of those who receive Jesus. You preach Jesus to these people living without Christ through an interpreter because you do not speak their language. At the conclusion of your preaching you *"...give an altar call..."* asking people to accept Jesus. A certain number of them come forward and repeat the words you give your interpreter for them to say.

You gather the people who come forward into a certain place after you have closed the main meeting. You congratulate them and tell them they are now saved. You encourage them about how they are the seed for a new local assembly. You instruct them to come to a certain building you have rented on a certain day for their first church meeting.

The people begin to gather regularly to meet as the members of the new local assembly. You provide instructions about *"...discipleship..."*. Days turn into weeks, and weeks turn into months. The people continue to live the same way they lived before you arrived. You become discouraged. No amount of prayer or fasting makes conditions any better. Nothing you do changes the conditions of the local assembly.

Making of a Ministry Gift

There are at least two possible endings for this narrative. The first involves the people of this foreign land simply *"...falling away..."* until there is no one left in the local assembly. At such a time the minister will then do one of two things. He will either tell himself he needs to be patient and will stay there for years witnessing no more changes than he has already seen. The other possibility, he will return to his homeland telling his supporters the people of the foreign land have rejected the *"...gospel...".*

Scripture makes it clear there are going to be some people some places who actually do reject the gospel *(Matthew 10:10-15)*. Under these conditions Jesus gives precise instructions what He expects of His ministers *(Matthew 10:14,15)*. Before *"...shaking off the dust from your feet...",* we must be certain that what the people have rejected was actually the *"...gospel...".* Paul wrote to the church at Corinth about his ministry to them.

> *"And I, brethren, when I came to you, did not come with excellence of speech or of wisdom declaring to you the testimony of God. For I determined not to know anything among you except Jesus Christ and Him crucified. I was with you in weakness, in fear, and in much trembling. And **my speech and my preaching were not with persuasive words of human wisdom, but in demonstration of the Spirit and of power, that your faith should not be in the wisdom of men but in the power of God.**"*
> *I Corinthians 2:1-5*

The gospel must not be preached with persuasive words of human wisdom but with demonstration of the Spirit and of power so the people's faith will be in the power of God and not the wisdom of men. It is not that difficult to see the difference between the true gospel and the traditions and doctrine of men.

I witnessed a wedding ceremony for two members of a local assembly in a land far, far away. Although the village was made up of grass houses with no electricity, a special type of organ was brought into the village to play *"Here Comes the Bride"*, and the bride wore a long white wedding dress. Helping two members of a local assembly enter the state of holy matrimony in no way requires an organ playing *"Here Comes the Bride"* or the wearing of a long white wedding dress.

The bride and groom, who wore traditional garb on a daily basis, said they wanted the bride to wear the long white dress and the organ to play because it was the Christian way, and they wanted God's blessing on their marriage. These components are simply traditions of men, not a part of the *"...gospel..."*. To reject the organ and the long white dress would certainly not have been rejecting the *"...gospel..."*.

In an opposite manner, I partook of Holy Communion with a people in a remote village. The meat of a green coconut was the *"...bread..."* and the coconut's milk was the *"...wine..."!* It was one of the most powerful times of communion of my personal life. Communion is not a tradition requiring a special type of bread and wine as elements but an expression of faith and submission to Jesus as Lord to remember His death! When done in faith, it is holy. When done only as a tradition, it is just a tradition.

Making of a Ministry Gift

The second possible ending for this narrative is for the minister to consult with his interpreter, a man from this particular area. Even though by now the minister is speaking the people's language in some measure, he cannot understand a lot of spiritual terms so consulting with his interpreter is a wise decision. The interpreter's input is sought because he is from the same area as the people of the local assembly, the language of the people is also his mother tongue, and the minister believes the interpreter can provide insights that a foreigner would not have.

The minister asks the interpreter for his input regarding the salvation experience of the people and why he believes they are not growing. What the interpreter tells the minister sends the minister reeling. The interpreter says the people came forward when the minister gave the *"...altar call..."* out of respect for him as a foreigner. They repeated the words the minister gave the interpreter for them to repeat in honor of the minister. In short, the people were not truly receiving Jesus, but merely participating in a ceremony. The people had not received or rejected the *"...gospel...".* They were just responding to words they had heard coming out of a man's mouth.

Certain scribes and Pharisees challenged Jesus regarding His disciples eating bread without first washing their hands. Jesus' reply was amazing.

> *"Then the scribes and Pharisees who were from Jerusalem came to Jesus, saying, Why do Your disciples transgress the tradition of the elders? For they do not wash their hands when they eat bread. He answered and said*

> to them, Why do you also transgress the commandment of God because of your tradition? For God commanded, saying,
>
>> 'Honor your father and your mother'; and
>> 'He who curses father or mother, let him be put to death.'
>
> But you say,
>
>> 'Whoever says to his father or mother, Whatever profit you might have received from me is a gift to God -- 'then he need not honor his father or mother.'
>
> Thus you have made the commandment of God of no effect by your tradition. Hypocrites! Well did Isaiah prophesy about you, saying:
>
>> 'These people draw near to Me with their mouth, and honor Me with their lips, but their heart is far from Me, and in vain they worship Me, teaching as doctrines the commandments of men.'
>> **Matthew 15:7,8**

Jesus called them *"...hypocrites..."* saying Isaiah's prophecy of a *"...people drawing near to God with their mouth and honoring Him with their lips, but their heart is far from Him..."* identified these very scribes and Pharaisees. Jesus was not calling them hypocrites because of His skills of spiritual discernment but, rather, because of the fruit of their lives. He could **"...see..."** the way they lived.

Earlier in the gospel written by Matthew Jesus was recorded as saying,

> "Beware of false prophets, who come to you in sheep's clothing, but inwardly they are ravenous wolves. You will know them by their fruits. Do men gather grapes from thornbushes or figs from thistles? Even so, every good tree bears good fruit, but a bad tree bears bad fruit. A good tree cannot bear bad fruit, nor can a bad tree bear good fruit. Every tree that does not bear good fruit is cut down and thrown into the fire. Therefore **by their fruits you will know them.**" **Matthew 7:15-20**

Jesus' words here represent revelation He desires for us to have, not just to identify false prophets, but as a tool for helping us to identify the fruit of everyone with whom we relate. We must know the people with whom we are involved. The "*...gospel...*" includes the ability God provides as the means for us to live in the new covenant. Jesus is revealing to us in clear and precise terms how we are to know one another: by the fruit of our lives. This is one of the abilities God is giving us to be able to live succesfully as the church. It does not require mature skills of discernment but, rather, simple sight as we look with our heart at the "*...fruit...*" born by one another.

We can enter an orchard and easily identify the difference between an apple and a peach just by looking at the fruit on each tree. This is exactly what Jesus did regarding the scribes and Pharisees. Jesus looked at the lives of the scribes and Pharisees and saw how they had created their own tradition making what they knew to be the word of God of no effect. He considered the fruit on their tree and called them hypocrites because of what He saw.

Another Gospel

Preaching the gospel to a lost people living bound in darkness and sin is the will of God. If the people to whom we have preached say they accept Christ but never demonstrate any change and continue to live lives of darkness and sin, it is the will of God for us to know them by their fruit. When Paul addressed the issue of the church living as mere men at Corinth, he had not identified their condition on the basis of his skill of spiritual discernment but, rather, what he could see as the fruit of their lives. It was no different than if he had picked an apple and called it an apple. He saw carnal, and he called it carnal. The *"...gospel..."* is not only the revelation of Jesus as the Lamb of God given to take away the sin of the world. It is also that God has designed the new covenant based on the ability He provides us rather than our own abilities. Knowing them by their fruit is part of those provisions. The enemy has labored endlessly to take this provision away from us in an effort to give us *another gospel*. The true gospel provision is *"...by their fruits you will know them..."* **(Matthew 7:20)**!

Making of a Ministry Gift

Chapter Six

Teams, Teams, Teams

There are three extremely similar Scriptural accounts of Jesus sending out His twelve most intimate disciples during His earthly ministry *(Matthew 10:1-ff; Mark 6:7-13; and Luke 9:1-6)*. Although each account is slightly different, the similarities in all three make them appear to be records of the same sending.

Mark's record provides us with a very important piece of information needed to help develop our understanding regarding teams.

> *"And He called the twelve to Himself, and began to **send them out two by two**, and gave them power over unclean spirits. He commanded them to take nothing for their journey except a staff -- no bag, no bread, no copper in their money belts -- but to wear sandals, and not to put on two tunics. Also He said to them,*
>
>> *'In whatever place you enter a house, stay there till you depart from that place. And whoever will not receive you nor hear you, when you depart from there, shake off the dust under your feet as a testimony against them. Assuredly, I say to you, it will be more tolerable for Sodom and Gomorrah in the day of judgment than for that city!'*
>
> *So they went out and preached that people should repent. And they cast out many demons, and anointed with oil many who were sick, and healed them."*
>
> **Mark 6:7-13**

Making of a Ministry Gift

Although neither *Matthew* nor *Luke's* record describes sending the disciples out in teams, *Mark's* record of this type of *"...team ministry..."* is consistent with other ministry throughout the New Testament.

The *Book of Ecclesiastes* was written by a person who identified himself as *"...the Preacher, the son of David, king in Jerusalem..." (Ecclesiastes 1:1)*. The *"...Preacher..."* is commonly accepted to be Solomon. Whether Solomon is the writer or not, we do not know for sure, but we can all agree *Ecclesiastes* is Scripture and, as such, is inspired by God the Holy Spirit. Whatever revelation is given in *Ecclesiastes*, we can receive it as divinely inspired.

> *"**Two are better than one**, because they have a good reward for their labor. For if they fall, one will lift up his companion. But woe to him who is alone when he falls, for he has no one to help him up. Again, if two lie down together, they will keep warm; but how can one be warm alone? Though one may be overpowered by another, two can withstand him. And a threefold cord is not quickly broken."* **Ecclesiastes 4:9,10**

These two verses in *Ecclesiastes* provide a wonderful premise as the basis to consider team ministry: ***Two are better than one!***

As part of Jesus' instructions to the twelve when he sent them out, He included a warning.

> *"Behold, **I send you out as sheep in the midst of wolves**. Therefore be wise as serpents and harmless as doves. But beware of men, for they will deliver you up to councils and scourge you in their synagogues..."*
> *Matthew 10:16-17*

Teams, Teams, Teams

Because Jesus was sending His disciples into harm's way, sending them out as teams based on the premise found in *Ecclesiastes 4:9,10* would have afforded them the best opportunity for safety and success. This *"...team ministry..."* format recorded by **Mark** was the provision and will of the Lord, at least for the disciples in the account recorded by **Mark**.

However, there are many illustrations of such teams throughout the New Testament. Peter and John *(Acts 3:1-4:19; Acts 8:14-25)*; Barnabas and Saul *(Acts 11:19-26; Acts 12:25; Acts 13:2-12)*; Paul and Barnabas *(Acts 13:42-14:13; Acts 15:1- 16:35)*; Paul and Silas *(Acts 15:39-17:12)* just to name a few. In addition to these *"...traveling teams..."* we see this same team concept in other types of ministry including the writing of epistles and corporate settings in local assemblies.

In letters written to the churches at Corinth, Philippi, Colosse, and Thessalonica, the opening greeting contains the names of Paul and other ministers.

> *"**Paul, an apostle of Jesus Christ by the will of God, and Timothy our brother**, to the church of God which is at Corinth, with all the saints who are in all Achaia..."*
> **II Corinthians 1:1**

> *"**Paul and Timothy**, bondservants of Jesus Christ, to all the saints in Christ Jesus who are in Philippi, with the bishops and deacons..."* **Philippians 1:1**

> *"**Paul, an apostle of Jesus Christ by the will of God, and Timothy our brother**, to the saints and faithful brethren in Christ who are in Colosse..."* **Colossians 1:1**

Making of a Ministry Gift

> *"**Paul, Silvanus, and Timothy**, to the church of the Thessalonians in God the Father and the Lord Jesus Christ..."* **I Thessalonians 1:1**

It is clear Paul was the lead minister in the writing of these letters. And, although these first verses are most representative of the greeting of a letter, they *"...indicate..."* that Paul saw his ministry as part of a team rather than just an individual ministering alone. He was certainly willing to include the name of other ministers in the greeting of these letters signifying the letter was also from them.

Philip, a man identified as *"...Philip the evangelist..."* in Scripture *(Acts 21:8)*, went down to the city of Samaria after persecution dispersed the disciples from Jerusalem *(Acts 8:1-5)* and preached Christ. Scripture declares, *"...the multitudes with one accord heeded the things spoken by Philip..." (Acts 8:6)*. In this context Scripture identifies the presence of more than one minister *(in this case apostles)* in the corporate setting from which Philip had come *(Acts 6:1-7; Acts 8:14)* .

> *"Now when **the apostles who were at Jerusalem** heard that Samaria had received the word of God, they sent Peter and John to them, who when they had come down prayed for them that they might receive the Holy Spirit..."*
> **Acts 8:14,15**

In other places in Scripture more than one minister was present in the corporate setting. In one such setting the *"...ministry team..."* Barnabas and Saul was indentified among the other ministries present.

Teams, Teams, Teams

> *"And Barnabas and Saul returned from Jerusalem when they had fulfilled their ministry, and they also took with them John whose surname was Mark. Now in the church that was at Antioch there were certain prophets and teachers: Barnabas, Simeon who was called Niger, Lucius of Cyrene, Manaen who had been brought up with Herod the tetrarch, and Saul. As they ministered to the Lord and fasted, the Holy Spirit said,*
>
> > *'Separate to Me Barnabas and Saul for the work to which I have called them.'*
>
> *Then, having fasted and prayed, and laid hands on them, they sent them away."* **Acts 12:25-13:3**

There is ample Scriptural evidence that many ministers functioned as *"...teams..."* in the New Testament. Perhaps we need to consider a very important question in this matter, *"Why would anyone rather minister to the people of the world alone or stand alone in the task of helping to perfect the saints in any setting?"* No minister should be looking for a loop-hole as the means of avoiding *"...team ministry..."*. All ministers should be eager to reap the benefits of other gifted and called ministers to help in all types of ministry.

Team ministry was the type of ministry which settled the dispute over the issue of circumcision *(Acts 15:1-29)*. In this portion of Scripture when the issue of circumcision arose in the church at Antioch producing *"...no small dissension and dispute with them, they determined that Paul and Barnabas and certain others should go up to Jerusalem, to the apostles and elders about this question...." (Acts 15:2)*. After Paul and Barnabas revealed the issue, a dispute erupted even in Jerusalem. However, they were able to achieve agreement on the matter and wrote a letter to the Gentile believers with instructions how to resolve the issue *(Acts 15:13-29)*.

In another Scriptural account a team of prophets traveled from Jerusalem to Antioch. One of the prophets of this team named Agabus provided ministry to the church foretelling a famine which was to come. The believers at Antioch were able to *"...send relief to the brethren dwelling in Judea..."* **(Acts 11:27-30)** in anticipation of what was to come.

We must not try to *"...create a case..."* for team ministry, but we also must not ignore the Scriptural accounts of teams of ministers identified by name producing such wonderful results. Having traveled to more than thirty five different nations over the span of thirty five plus years, I have traveled both alone and as a part of a team. If teams of ministers are in agreement regarding doctrine, modes of travel, and accommodations in the foreign setting, teams are by far the easiest and most productive method of ministry.

One recurring issue involving teams on every level seems to be the primary *"...nemesis..."* of team ministry: **Who is in charge?** The only solution plausible is the architecture of the Lord! From the creation of Adam and Eve, to the anointing of Kings, to ministry teams, the Lord has a will for who is in charge, if anyone is to be in charge. Adam was designed to be the governmental head over Eve; Kings in the old covenant were anointed to rule over the people of God, but what about ministry teams, especially a team of just two ministers? Is it the Lord's will for one minister to provide leadership for the

Teams, Teams, Teams

team of two ministers who are both called to the same office of ministry laboring together?

Consider the ministry team of Paul and Barnabas. Shortly after Saul of Tarsus' Damascus Road experience where he met the Lord Jesus and subsequently submitted to Jesus' Lordship and to his calling to the ministry, Saul endeavored to join the disciples in Jerusalem.

> *"And **when Saul had come to Jerusalem, he tried to join the disciples; but they were all afraid of him, and did not believe that he was a disciple.** But Barnabas took him and brought him to the apostles. And he declared to them how he had seen the Lord on the road, and that He had spoken to him, and how he had preached boldly at Damascus in the name of Jesus. So he was with them at Jerusalem, coming in and going out..."*
> **Acts 9:26-28**

After a certain amount of time, Barnabas found Saul and took him to Antioch where they remained for an entire year teaching the disciples. Scripture says it was here at Antioch the disciples were first called Christians *(Acts 11:26)*. Evidently this time of ministry over the period of the year cemented them together as a ministry team. Scripture referred to them as Barnabas and Saul *(Acts 12:25)*. Even the Holy Spirit referred to them as *Barnabas and Saul* in a prophetic utterance spoken through one of the ministers in Antioch *(Acts 13:2)*.

> *"Now **separate to Me Barnabas and Saul for the work to which I have called them.** Then having fasted and prayed, and laid hands on them, they sent them away. So, being sent out by the Holy Spirit, they went down to Seleucia, and from there they sailed to Cyprus...."*
> ***Acts 13:2-4***

Making of a Ministry Gift

The Holy Spirit not only identified a new phase of ministry for Barnabas and Saul at the same time and in the same setting, but also sent them out together. Part of the prophetic utterance inspired by the Holy Spirit used the pronoun *"...them..." (Acts 13:2)*, signifying in some manner the Holy Spirit saw them together. I suppose it could be said this was simply an ordination service where two ministers were being ordained to the same office of apostle and, then, being sent out to fulfill their individual ministries. However, when Barnabas and Saul traveled to the same places and were received together by the people in those places, it is beyond coincidence. They were a team.

Then a strange thing began to occur. What was initially Barnabas and Paul changed. *Acts 13:13* identifies the team as *"...Paul and his company..."*. *Acts 13:50* again identifies Paul's name first in his relationship with Barnabas as *"...Paul and Barnabas..."*. Coincidence? Or is something happening which is identifying a new role relationship developing between these two ministers?

One Sabbath they entered the synagogue, and after the reading of the Law and the Prophets, one of the rulers of the synagogue said,

> *"...Men and brethren, if you have any word of exhortation for the people, say on. Then Paul stood up, and motioning with his hand said, 'Men of Israel, and you who fear God, listen:..."* **Acts 13:15-following**

Teams, Teams, Teams

Paul spoke the word of God at length. The very next Sabbath, when nearly the whole city turned out to hear the word of God, the Jews became envious and controversy arose. It is in this setting that Paul declared *"...their..." (Paul & Barnabas')* ministry was to the Gentiles.

> *"Then Paul and Barnabas grew bold and said,*
>
> > *'It was necessary that the word of God should be spoken to you first; but since you reject it, and judge yourselves unworthy of everlasting life, behold, we turn to the Gentiles.* ***For so the Lord has commanded us****:*
> >
> > > *'I have set you as a light to the Gentiles, that you should be for salvation to the ends of the earth.'* **Acts 13:46,47**

Paul and Barnabas then traveled to Iconium and on to Lystra. In Lystra a major miracle occurred and a major clue was given about the role relationship between Paul and Barnabas.

> *"And in Lystra a certain man without strength in his feet was sitting, a cripple from his mother's womb, who had never walked. This man heard Paul speaking. Paul, observing him intently and seeing that he had faith to be healed, said with a loud voice,*
>
> > *'Stand up straight on your feet!'*
>
> *And he leaped and walked. Now when the people saw what Paul had done, they raised their voices, saying in the Lycaonian language,*
>
> > *'The gods have come down to us in the likeness of men!'*

Making of a Ministry Gift

And Barnabas they called Zeus, **and Paul, Hermes,** *because he was the chief speaker..." Acts 14:8-12*

Even the people of the world could see that Paul was the chief speaker. How was this role established? Was Paul just pushy, jumping up to speak first before Barnabas had a chance? Or could it have been the inspiration from the Anointing resident inside of Paul that motivated him to speak and the Anointing inside of Barnabas that motivated him to accept Paul's role as from God?

There is no Scripture which establishes the truth in this matter. However, it seems clear that Paul was the chief speaker between him and Barnabas, whether in the synagogue or in the world. The exact time frame is not clear, but *Acts 14:36-39* says a dispute between Paul and Barnabas over John Mark, a young disciple, was so sharp they departed from one another. We never hear of their names in a team context again. And we do not know if Paul's role had any influence on their division. Scripture only tells us their departure from one another was over the issue of John Mark. Shortly after the division between them, Paul and Silas began to walk together as an apostolic team.

There is a really strong Scriptural base upon which to sit *"...team ministry..."*. Even if we only apply the wisdom found in *Ecclesiastes 4:9,10* *"...two are better than one..."* we just have to ask the question again, *"Why would anyone rather minister to the people of the world alone or stand alone in the task of helping to perfect the saints in any setting?"* Every single person gifted and called to any of the offices of ministry needs to be considering how to most effectively reach the people of the world and how to see the saints perfected. **Team ministry** is a wonderful provision to help with both of these holy endeavors!

Chapter Seven

Idealism, Tradition, & The Will of God

The difference between idealism, tradition, and the will of God is enormous. ***Idealism***, ***ideal***, and ***idealist*** are defined by **Webster's New Universal Unabridged Dictionary** as...

idealism

> behavior or thought based on a conception of things as they should be or as one would wish them to be; idealization.

ideal

> 1. a conception embodying perfection.
> 2. an object which corresponds with such a conception; a perfect model.
> 3. something which exists only in the mind; an imaginary object without fault, a flawless pattern, model, example, or standard.

idealist

> a person whose behavior or thought is based on ideals: often used contemptuously to mean an impractical visionary or dreamer

Idealism embodies the notion that the conception of things primarily exists only as a perfect standard or model in the mind of the way things should be. This notion in relation

Making of a Ministry Gift

to our God is not even remotely appropriate. God is not a figment of our imagination! He is very real! Believing our God exists is a fundamental operation of our faith.

> *"...he who comes to God must believe that He is (exists)..."* **Hebrews 11:6**

Tradition, too, as a foundational component for how we relate to our God is lacking. **Webster's New Universal Unabridged Dictionary** defines **tradition** as...

> ...a long-established custom or practice that has the effect of an unwritten law.

In one verbal exchange Jesus had with certain scribes and Pharisees regarding *"...tradition..."*, He quoted one of their traditions *(Matthew 15:1-9)* and then told them,

> *"...you have made the commandment of God of no effect by your **tradition**..."* **Matthew 15:6**

Although traditions handed down from men do not always *"...make the commandment of God of no effect..."*, they are lacking as the foundation upon which we must build our relationship with our God. Rather than basing our lives on tradition, we must establish our lives on our personal knowledge of God, His existence, and His Word!

Neither God nor His will are based on *"...ideals..."* or *"...traditions..."*! He really exists and His will is based solidly on His existence and His character! There is something so fundamental about the will of God based on the existence

Idealism, Tradition, Will of God

of God that it must become a foundational building block of our relationship with God! A person who refuses to acknowledge the existence of God will certainly not be willing to consider the will of God. Conversely, a person who believes in the existence of God should eagerly embrace the will of God. Consider an illustration from Scripture regarding man, God, and God's will:

> "By faith Noah, being divinely warned of things not yet seen, moved with godly fear, prepared an ark for the saving of his household, by which he condemned the world and became heir of the righteousness which is according to faith." **Hebrews 11:7**

Consider these Scriptural facts:
*(All taken from **Genesis Chapters Two, Five, & Seven**)*

1. *Noah did not know rain.*
2. *Noah heard God speak to him about the flood.*
3. *Noah followed God's instructions to build the ark. Noah saved*
4. *his family by doing the will of God.*
5. *Noah condemned the world by doing the will of God.*

Noah believed God existed and that God had a will in relation to man and the earth. None of these Scriptural facts are based on idealism or tradition. Noah knew God! It was his relationship with God and his knowledge of God's will which is based solidly on the existence and character of God that moved him to action.

We can consider the concepts of idealism and tradition one of two ways: The way man sees God, or the way we think God sees man. Noah's perspective of God was not idealistic

Making of a Ministry Gift

nor traditional. Noah believed God existed, and he believed God's will was real. God's perspective of man and the earth is most certainly not based on idealism. God is not idealistic nor traditional; He is God. However, history records many men have been deceived into thinking God and His will are based on ideals or traditions.

In the Scriptural account involving Noah, God had a *"...will..."* for the earth and for the men who were designed to inhabit it. When He considered the reality of the condition of man and the earth, His desire was to re-establish His will for both. According to the definition of *"...idealism..."*, an idealistic God would have looked at the earth and the condition of man and said, *"Things are just the way they are. They are not as they should be or as I would wish them to be. They do not conform to the imagination of my mind."* However, God's will is not a wish nor an imagination. **His will is as real as He is!**

God's relationship with mankind prior to the giving of the new covenant was stringent and conclusive.

> "Then the Lord saw that the wickedness of man was great in the earth, and that every intent of the thoughts of his heart was only evil continually. And the Lord was sorry that He had made man on the earth, and He was grieved in His heart. So the Lord said,
>
>> 'I will destroy man whom I have created from the face of the earth, both man and beast, creeping thing and birds of the air, for I am sorry I have made them.'
>
> But Noah found grace in they eyes of the Lord."
>   ***Genesis 6:5-8***

Idealism, Tradition, Will of God

God saw His will had been violated, *"...that the wickedness of man was great in the earth, and that every intent of the thoughts of his heart was only evil continually...".* As a result, He made provision for His will to be restored.

There is no Scriptural reason given regarding the timing of God's actions. We can only speculate God did not move sooner because of His great love for mankind, and He was simply being patient and longsuffering, hoping man would change. However, we know God did move. Noah and the flood were God's will.

Every born again believer needs to understanding that neither God nor His will are based on ideals or traditions! God is real, and His will is real! Our God does not reveal His will to us as, *"This is what I would like for you to do. I know how hard it is going to be to do My will, so anything close to it will be okay. Just do the best you can."* This is absolutely not the way our God relates to us.

The end result of His will is typically not able to be realized all at once. Many aspects of His will require process to bring to pass. One such example would be, He wills for every single born again believer to grow in the knowledge of Him. This growth does not, cannot, happen all at once. A believer grows methodically toward maturity.

> *"As newborn babes, desire the pure milk of the word, that you may grow thereby."* **I Peter 2:2**

Making of a Ministry Gift

> *"Whom shall he teach knowledge? And whom will he make to understand the message? Those just weaned from milk? Those just drawn from the breasts? For precept must be upon precept, precept upon precept, line upon line, line upon line, here a little, there a little."*
> **Isaiah 28:9-10**

Any attempt to *"...speed up..."* the believer's growth will be counter-productive. Great patience, stewardship, monitoring, love, and care must be provided for each and every believer to help nurture him to maturity.

We do not want to fall into any of the enemy's traps enabling any of his devices. God did not redeem mankind to be His servants; He redeemed us to be His sons. Further, the Lord Jesus did not give the offices of ministry to raise up the sons of God to make them good servants. The offices of ministry have been given to provide knowledge of our God to the sons of God so God's sons may know Him and make Him known!

When God sent His only begotten Son into the earth to live as the Lamb of God to take away the sin of the world, this was only part of His sovereign plan. Crucifixion, death, burial, and resurrection were also parts of His plan. Paul's prayer for the church at Ephesus succinctly and most wonderfully expresses a comprehensive view of God's plan for His only begotten Son.

> *"After I heard of your faith in the Lord Jesus and your love for all the saints, do not cease to give thanks for you, making mention of you in my prayers: that the God of our Lord Jesus Christ, the Father of glory, may give*

Idealism, Tradition, Will of God

*to you the spirit of wisdom and revelation in the knowledge of Him, the eyes of your understanding being enlightened; that you may know what is the hope of His calling, what are the riches of the glory of His inheritance in the saints, and what is the exceeding greatness of His mighty power which He worked in Christ when He raised Him from the dead and seated Him at His right hand in the heavenly places, far above all principality and power and might and dominion, and every name that is named, not only in this age but also in that which is to come. And **He put all things under His feet, and gave Him to be head over all things to the church, which is His body, the fullness of Him who fills all in all.***"
Ephesians 1:15-23

Scripture states clearly here the Father willed for Jesus to be *"...head over all things to the church..."*. Paul wrote in this same letter to the church at Ephesus that Jesus *"...Himself gave the offices of ministry..." (Ephesians 4:11)*. How can there be any controversy regarding who gave the offices of ministry, whether Jesus had a right to give them, or the tenure of the offices of ministry? All of the ministries have been given *"...till we all come to the unity of the faith and of the knowledge of the Son of God, to a perfect man, to the measure of the stature of the fullness of Christ..." (Ephesians 4:13)*.

Surely we can establish agreement that the conditions stated in *Ephesians 4:13* are not yet fulfilled. However, even if someone wishes to be argumentative and say these conditions are met, that would make all of the offices of ministry no longer needed. The Lord did not limit the tenure of any of the offices. They are *"...all..."* included as having been given until all of the conditions of *Ephesians 4:13* are met.

Making of a Ministry Gift

Even if we limit the purposes of the offices of ministry only *"...for the perfecting of the saints for the work of ministry..." (NKJV)*, or *"...for the perfecting of the saints..." (KJV)*, Jesus *"...Himself gave some to be apostles, some prophets, some evangelists, and some pastors and teachers..." (Ephesians 4:11-13)* to fulfill these purposes. If this truly is His will, then we will never see these purposes fulfilled without the gifts He has given functioning accordingly. That is, the saints cannot reach *"...the knowledge of the Son of God, to a perfect man, to the measure of the stature of the fullness of Christ..."* separate and apart from the offices of ministry Christ has given for these purposes.

Any born again person who has shifted back to mere man minded cannot see the will of God correctly. Such a person will have little alternative but to *"...idealize..."* the will of God one way or another. However, the church is responsible to see ourselves as spiritual people, to receive the knowledge of God's will, and to seek God regarding how He intends for His will to be put into affect.

Summary & Conclusion

Two immutable characteristics of our God are His *"...giving..."* and His *"...love..."!* These ubiquitous characteristics of His are present in every part of His relationship with us. When the Word came to the earth, having divested Himself of His divine attributes to be clothed in flesh as the man Jesus, He still embodied these same characteristics. ***He loves us and He is a giver!*** Some of the gifts He has given because of His love for us are the offices of ministry. He gave these gifts to provide us with the knowledge of God as the means for us to partake of life like God has it.

Christ Jesus is preeminent in all things to the church. Neither the ministers nor the church's perspective of them must ever challenge Christ's preeminence. The enemy labors tirelessly to obscure our understanding of the offices of ministry, their proper placement, and role in the church. We are redeemed to be sons of God, but we enter the kingdom as babes in Christ. We are designed to grow in knowledge of God. It is this knowledge of God which causes us to increase in life like God has it unto maturity. The offices of ministry have been given to provide us with revelation knowledge of God so we may know Him, live in that knowledge, and make Him known.

Each office has a specific and unique revelation of Christ and a specific and unique work of ministry different from the other offices of ministry and from those who are not called to the offices. The knowledge we receive is not merely informational, but also revelational, designed to become skills as a way of life. The ministers are to help us translate the revelation they give us into the skills by which we are to live.

The *"...calling..."* of God to any of the offices of ministry is the only way a person can be an apostle, prophet, evangelist, pastor, or teacher. God is the One who calls a person to an office of ministry, and He is the One who makes that calling known to the person called. It may be through a prophetic utterance from another minister, but the initiative to make the calling known is from God. The calling of God is what makes a person an apostle, prophet, evangelist, pastor, or teacher, **not** what a person does in ministry. A person's work of ministry will be according to his calling, but calling first, then work of ministry.

Jeremiah was sanctified and ordained by God as a prophet before he was born. It was **not** his work as a prophet that made him a prophet, but rather the calling of God! A person is just as much an apostle, prophet, evangelist, pastor, or teacher at the beginning of his ministry as he is at the end. Hopefully, a person will be more skilled in his calling at the end of his ministry, but not more called. What you do in ministry does not determine your office of ministry. Your office of ministry determines what you do in ministry. God is the One who determines the office to which you are called!

We are designed to serve God but from a position of love and sonship rather than as servants. Our priority must be loving God as our Father rather than as our Master. The pri-

Summary & Conclusion

ority of His love for us is certainly as sons rather than as servants. Our knowledge of Christ as the Lamb of God sent to take away the sin of the world and our acceptance of Him as such is what made us sons. The fundamental building block of all ministry is to reveal Christ as the means of knowing Him, living by that knowledge, and making Him known.

Revelation of Christ is the primary component of ministers' offices. This revelation is the very basis for their ministries. The Lord Jesus has vested each office of ministry with certain equipment, revelation, and purpose. The offices of ministry are the *"...gifts..."* Christ has given, not the person standing in each office.

The gifts are not given in a vacuum, as builders or politicians in the natural world are not. They are designed to work together with other gifted and called ministers in order to produce the results Christ has ordained. The goal of revealing Christ to everyone so they may know Him to either be saved or grow to maturity is simply impossible for any one person alone. Ministers must learn to work together to see our results increase.

The most important component of equipment for the offices of ministry is the Anointing who is the Holy Spirit. While there are a diversity of manifestations of the Holy Spirit, there is only one Holy Spirit. Because the Holy Spirit is also the Anointing, and even though there are a diversity of manifestations of the Anointing, there is still only One Anointing.

Making of a Ministry Gift

There is not an apostolic anointing, a prophetic anointing, an evangelistic anointing, a pastoral anointing, a teaching anointing, but *One Anointing* who simply manifests Himself differently as the ability of God each minister needs to fulfill his calling. Because the Anointing is a person who is God, our priority is to develop a *"...relationship..."* with the Anointing.

God the Holy Spirit, the Anointing, also provides ministers with the ability of God required to fulfill three ministerial functions common to all of the offices: The ability... 1) ...to procure and understand revelation of Christ appropriate to the office to which we are called... 2) ...to impart that revelation... 3) ...to *"...see..."* beyond the sight of a non-ministry individual believer into the *"...big picture..."* of the building process. These three things will help all ministers see the need to work together in this massive construction project building the temple of the Lord.

God's calling to an individual separates that individual to an office of ministry within the body of Christ, not from the body of Christ. The difference between these two notions is the difference between ministers serving the sons of God to ministers being served by the sons of God. Ministers are to serve the sons of God, not the other way around!

The Lord Jesus has assigned the responsibility to steward the mysteries of God to ministers. This responsibility requires the person called to minister appropriate revelation to the saints according to their level of spiritual growth, to monitor the progress of the saints, and to build on the revelation already given by other ministers.

Summary & Conclusion

The value of the saints is established by who the saints are as the sons of God, not by what they do. A performance based value system is not the way of God! Truly what we do is of great value to our God, but *"...our..."* value is determined on the basis of who we are!

If a believer is taught that God loves him no matter what he does without also being taught that what he does has great bearing on the quality of life he lives, he will easily fall victim to one of the enemy's devices. Love and performance are not **either or**. They are *"...God loves me for who I am..."*, **and** *"...God cares about my performance because it has great bearing on the quality of life I live..." (i.e. **Romans 6:16**)!* While our performance has great bearing on the quality of life we live, it does not alter God's love for us. He loves us even if we choose to live in sin after new birth. However, our choice causes us to live a life of bondage even with God loving us. The stewardship responsibilities of ministers helps the saints understand this truth.

The gospel includes revelation of Jesus as the means of being saved and the ability of God as the means of living in the new covenant after salvation! The enemy knows he most likely cannot strip away God's saving grace from us so he tries to deceive us into believing it is really, really hard to do the will of God after salvation. Anytime this notion comes to you, the device of the enemy will always be involved. It is not *"...hard..."* to do the will of God; it is *"...impossible..."* for natural man in his own ability to do the will of God.

Making of a Ministry Gift

The old covenant was based on man's ability. The new covenant is based on God's ability given to man. Whatever God reveals to the church today as His will, we can be confident it is in His ability that we will be able to do His will! Do not accept *"...another gospel..."* which emphasizes how difficult it is to do the will of God. The true gospel is good news about Jesus as the means to be saved *and* the ability God gives us as the means of receiving Jesus in order to be born again and of doing His will in the new covenant after new birth!

When Jesus sent His disciples out *"...two by two...",* He was installing a tool of ministry to help provide for ministers' safety and success: **Teams!** The writer of the **Book of Ecclesiastes** wrote by inspiration of God the Holy Spirit *"...two are better than one...".* There is ample Scriptural evidence for *"...teams..."* in the New Testament. Why would anyone rather minister to the people of the world alone or stand alone in the task of helping to perfect the saints? All ministers should be eager to reap the benefits of other gifted and called ministers to help in all types of ministry.

Idealism and tradition are both lacking for how we relate to our God. Our relationship with our God must be based on personal knowledge of God, His existence, and His word! The will of God is based solidly on His existence and His character. A person who refuses to acknowledge His existence will certainly not be willing to consider His will. However, a person who believes in the existence of God should eagerly embrace the will of God.

Summary & Conclusion

Neither God nor His will are based on ideals or traditions. **God is real, and His will is real!** Whatever our God wills for us, that is *"...really..."* what He wills! Seeing ourselves as spiritual people, the church is responsible to receive knowledge of God's will and seek Him regarding how He intends for His will to be put into effect.

Suppose the Lord gives you the task of pioneering ministry to a nation of people who have never heard of Jesus. It would seem like such a daunting task you may become discouraged even before you begin. Perhaps there is something we can learn from a natural world illustration. There is an old adage asking, *"How do you eat an elephant?"* Of course the typical answer is, *"One bite at a time!"* The adage and its conclusion can be applied to almost any task which presents itself in a daunting manner.

However, I recently read a very insightful article written several years ago challenging the typical response of *"One bite at a time."* The writer's challenge was, instead of asking *"How do you eat an elephant?"*, a better question would be *"Why would you want to eat an elephant?"* This new question opens the door to a marvelous insight which, when applied, could help a person avoid the proto-typical traps involved with huge projects. Perhaps the most devastating of these traps is to try to remain motivated through the entire long-term project.

If we apply these *"...insights..."* derived from the better question of *"Why would you want to eat an elephant?"* to the task of pioneering ministry to a nation of people who have never heard of Jesus, the conclusion is truly remarkable. If our goal is to reach the entire nation, that is a good goal. But, the challenge lies in the enormous long-term proposition of the task. However, if we ask *"Why does the Lord want the people of this nation to hear of Jesus"*, perhaps this will help us begin to see the task from a different, better perspective.

The Lord would send us to the nation so that every single person in the nation might have opportunity to be saved and experience eternal life. We would rejoice whenever any *"...one..."* person entered into salvation. Surely we could find strength, courage, and motivation to continue on assignment because of the great joy gained when individuals began receiving Jesus on a regular basis.

Now, in comparison, *"Why does the Lord want the entire church to understand the giving, calling, and functioning of the offices of ministry?"* **Because they are His provision to perfect the saints!** Jesus' purpose for giving these offices of ministry is so those called can give others the revelation they have been given as the means of entering the kingdom and growing to maturity!

> *No matter how daunting the task may seem, we must give accurate revelation and understanding to the church regarding the offices Christ has given to perfect the saints!*

www.ingramcontent.com/pod-product-compliance
Lightning Source LLC
Chambersburg PA
CBHW071310060426
42444CB00034B/1759